Barcelona

Front cover: Facade of Casa Batlló at twilight

Right: La Sagrada Família's four towers

TOP 10 ATTRACTIONS

La Rambla • A lively and entertaining place by day or night *(page 23)*

Sagrada Família • Work continues on Gaudí's unfinished masterpiece *(page 53)*

Fundació Joan Miró • This museum showcases an exceptional body of the artist's work *(page 67)*

The Monestir de Pedralbes • A peaceful haven *(page 70)*

Casa Batlló • One of the stunning *modernista* buildings for which the city is famous *(page 48)*

The Museu Picasso • The largest collection of the artist's work ouside Paris *(page 43)*

Palau de la Música Catalana • An explosion of mosaics, tiles and sculpture *(page 45)*

The Palau Nacional • This beautiful palace houses some of Catalonia's greatest works of art *(page 64)*

The Barri Gòtic • The sombre Gothic Cathedral is at the heart of this old quarter *(page 30)*

The Waterfront • A raft of new beaches make this a playground for the local people *(page 56)*

CONTENTS

46

62

25

32

89
57

INTRODUCTION

Barcelona may be the second city of Spain, locked in eternal rivalry with Madrid, but it ruled an empire long before Spain was even born. Some 2,000 years ago, the Romans, on their way to conquering the whole of Iberia, built a forbidding wall around their settlement on the Mediterranean coast and called it Barcino.

Although a visitor could spend days wandering the Gothic Quarter, an atmospheric tangle of medieval buildings and alleyways where the city's glorious past is palpable, Barcelona is anything but a musty old history lesson. It is a dynamic, densely populated, and daringly modern metropolis. Since hosting the 1992 Olympic Games, the city, capital of the autonomous region of Catalonia, has become one of Europe's hottest cities.

Once grimy and grey, with a smelly industrial port that pushed this former maritime power away from the sea, Barcelona has reinvented itself. Badly needed new circulation routes were built, rundown neighbourhoods have been reborn and numerous 'urban spaces', featuring sculpture and greenery, have been created. The airport, railway and Metro have been brought up to date, and new hotels, museums and concert halls have sprung up. The most important physical change, though, has been Barcelona's reorientation towards the sea. With a newly dynamic port that is now one of the busiest cruise-ship stops in Europe, the Olimpic port and a further new leisure port at Diagonal Mar, with its clean urban beaches, and renowned seafront neighbourhoods, the Catalan capital has succeeded in marrying the seductive pleasures of the Mediterranean with the sophisticated, creative energy of modern Europe.

The elegant Plaça Reial is always full of life

Catalan Culture

Barcelona's physical transformation has accompanied a re-
birth of Catalan culture, long marginalised – often overtly
repressed – by Spanish rulers. The most ruthless aggression
came during the Franco dictatorship, whichlasted from the
Spanish Civil War of 1936–39, until the dictator's death in
1975. Under the 1979 Statute of Autonomy, Catalonia re-
gained a substantial measure of self government; this was
moderately amplified by a new statute approved in 2006.
Catalan arts, literature and language, are vigorously promoted by the Catalan government.

**Street music can be heard at
any time of the day**

Reawakened, too, is the
pride the Barceloneses take in
their city. They are proud of
their architecture and design.
The man behind much of it
is the city's most famous son,
Antoni Gaudí (1852–1926),
one of the creators of *modernisme*, Catalan Art Nouveau. Gaudí's buildings still
startle: his soaring, un-
finished cathedral, La Sagrada Família, is his best-known
work, but there are scores
more in Barcelona. And
that's just Gaudí; around the
turn of the 20th century, a
group of *modernistas*, including Lluís Domènech i
Montaner and Josep Puig i
Cadafalch, dreamed up the
most fanciful buildings their
rich imaginations and equal-

ly rich patrons would allow. More recent architectural stars include Oriol Bohigas, Santiago Calatrava, Miralles and Tagliabue and a host of international architects like Jean Nouvel, Norman Foster and Richard Rogers, who are all creating new landmarks in the city.

Take a tour

To quickly get the full measure of this dynamic Mediterranean city hop on (and off wherever you want) the Bus Turístic, or go for a walking, bike, boat, scooter or helicopter tour. Check <www.barcelonaturisme. com> for the latest offers.

Design and Pragmatism

Barcelona also nurtured the careers of some of the 20th-century's greatest artists – the Catalans Joan Miró and Salvador Dalí, and also Pablo Picasso, who spent his formative years in the Catalan capital before seeking fame in Paris (Barcelona's Picasso museum has the largest collection of his work outside Paris). Few other cities are as design-mad as Barcelona. The opening of every high-tech museum, bridge and bar is a public event discussed and debated by local people. Thirty thousand people visited Richard Meier's Museum of Contemporary Art (MACBA) on its first weekend, though there was scarcely a work of art in the place. Couples rush to place their wedding lists at the trendiest design shops, and avant-garde public spaces are analysed thoughtfully and, more often than not, publicly funded.

However, Barceloneses tend to be surprisingly conservative and pragmatic. Spain's industrial juggernaut, Barcelona is serious about work and money. With 15 percent of Spain's population (1.7 million in the city itself), Catalonia produces more than 20 percent of the country's GDP and a quarter of all exports. Catalans have a reputation for being tight with money – a criticism that's a backhanded compliment acknowledging that they know how to earn and manage it.

Linguistic Differences

Barcelona has long been considered different from the rest of Spain, and though visitors can attend a bullfight or flamenco show, this really isn't the place for such typically Spanish practices. The city is famous for its stubborn sense of independence and identity. Catalans have held onto their language tenaciously, defending it against repeated attempts from Castile, and the Franco government, to extinguish it. Above all, they believe Catalonia is a nation, not a mere region. You will see T-shirts proclaiming that 'Catalunya is not Spain', and hear shopkeepers responding to Spanish speakers in Catalan – bilingual conversations that can be harmless or political, depending upon the participants. While there are many who would prefer Barcelona to be the capital of an independent, Catalan-speaking nation, the majority of these hard-working people are simply frustrated that so much locally generated wealth is re-routed to Madrid.

All political considerations are cast aside, though, when seemingly the whole of Barcelona takes to the streets just before lunch or in the early evening. La Rambla, a tree-lined boulevard Victor Hugo called 'the most beautiful in the

Sardanes

The city – and the region – takes its culture seriously. Rituals like the *sardana*, a traditional dance performed on Saturday evening and Sunday morning in front of the cathedral, and in Plaça Sant Jaume on some Sunday evenings, are held almost sacred. Men, women and children hold hands and form a circle to perform the apparently simple but highly regimented steps. The band, called a *cobla*, comprising strings, brass and a drum, plays lilting, melancholic tunes as more and more circles form until the entire area is filled with dedicated dancers.

Plaça del Sardana in Monjuïc

world', is packed with local people and visitors. Boisterous patrons spill out of corner bars, where they've dipped in to eat tapas (an array of snacks that might include a wedge of omelette, sardines, octopus, olives, cheese, chorizo sausage and much more) and have a glass of wine, beer or local cava (sparkling wine that comes from just outside Barcelona). Mime artists strike poses for photos and spare change, and older people take a seat to watch the whole parade stream by.

Exploring on Foot

Take your cue from local people and La Rambla: Barcelona is an ideal city for walking. Hemmed in by the sea and hills on three sides, the city is surprisingly manageable. It spills down a gentle slope to the waterfront. Near the water is the Barri Gòtic (Gothic Quarter) and the rest of the old city, a labyrinth of streets inhabited for a thousand years. Ancient stones of the Roman city are visible in columns and walls, and in underground passages – the settlement's original foundations – you can visit beneath the Museu d'Història de la Ciutat. Barcelona grew out of its original walls, and its modern sectors extend in all directions. There are only a handful of high-rise buildings, and the avenues are broad and leafy, punctuated by squares crowded with cafés. The Eixample district, a grid of streets laid out in the 19th century, includes landmark *modernista* apartment buildings, fashionable boutiques, galleries, restaurants and hotels.

Barcelona is every bit as spirited at night as it is during the day. Residents begin their evenings with tapas and rounds of drinks after work, activities that put dinner off until a fashionably late hour. Ten o'clock is normal but it's not uncommon for Barceloneses to sit down to dinner at midnight. Live-music venues and discos don't really get going until 2am. Any day of the week, La Rambla pulsates with life into the early hours of the morning. If late-night Barcelona is too wild for your tastes, an evening stroll is also a highlight: the cathedral and other churches, palaces and monuments, are all illuminated. The Barri Gòtic retreats into silence, broken only by the sharp sounds of a family quarrel or the animated hollering of late-night revellers.

The leafy Rambla cuts through the centre of the city

A BRIEF HISTORY

Barcelona was originally called Barcino, named after the Carthaginian general and father of Hannibal, Hamilcar Barca, who established a base on the northeastern coast of Iberia in c.300BC. Phoenicians and Greeks had previously settled the area, and Barcino occupied the site of an earlier Celtiberian settlement called Laie. But the Romans, who conquered all of Iberia, left the most indelible marks on Barcelona. They defeated the Carthaginians in 197BC and ruled Spain for the next 600 years, a period in which Roman law, language and culture took firm root across the peninsula. The Roman citadel in Barcelona, surrounded by a massive wall, occupied high ground where the cathedral and city hall now stand. From the 1st century AD Christian communities spread throughout Catalonia.

Visigothic Capital

After the sack of Rome Visigoths swept into Spain in AD476. They made Barcelona their capital from 531 until 554, when they moved their power base to Toledo. The invasion of the Moors in 713 brought the Visigothic kingdom to an end, and Catalonia was briefly overrun by the invaders from north Africa. After their defeat beyond the Pyrenees by the Franks in 801, the Moors withdrew to the south, and retained no lasting foothold in Catalonia. Charlemagne's knights installed themselves in the border counties to guard the southern flank of his empire.

Catalan character

While much of Spain was under Moorish domination, Catalonia remained linked to Europe. This has done much to determine the distinctive Catalan character.

Ramon Berenguer, who enlarged the Catalan nation

A feudal lord, Guifré el Pelós – Wilfred the Hairy – became the Count of Barcelona. In 878 he founded a dynasty that would rule for nearly five centuries. He also gave the budding nation its flag of four horizontal red stripes on a gold field, the oldest still in use in Europe. Legend holds that the stripes were etched in Wilfred's blood, drawn on his shield by the fingers of the Frankish king after the count had defended his overlord in a battle.

When King Louis V refused to come to their aid against Moorish raiders, the counts of Barcelona declared their independence in 988, a date celebrated as Catalonia's birth as a nation-state. The Catalan nation was soon enlarged through marriage and military adventure. Ramon Berenguer III, who ruled from 1082–1131, captured Mallorca, Ibiza and Tarragona from the Moors and acquired the French county of Provence through his wife. His successor, Ramon Berenguer IV, united Catalonia with neighbouring Aragón by marriage, and his son, Alfonso II, became the first joint king of Aragón and Catalonia and was known as 'the Emperor of the Pyrenees'.

Mercantile Nation

Successive generations turned their attention towards the conquest of the Mediterranean basin. Jaume I (1213–76) consolidated control over the Balearic Islands and claimed Valencia. Sicily was annexed in 1282 and over the ensuing century, Barcelona reached the peak of its glory. Its mercantilist trade grew rapidly and its territories included Sardinia, Corsica, Naples and the Roussillon in southern France.

The Middle Ages, from the late 13th to the 15th century, were a time of great building in Barcelona, giving rise to the cathedral and other great Gothic palaces and monuments. Barcelona served as a channel for the exchange of scientific knowledge and scholarship. The arts flourished, patronised by a vigorous class of artisans, bankers and merchants, including an important Jewish community.

Nascent political institutions appeared, and in 1359 the Corts Catalanes, or Catalan parliament, which had been meeting irregularly since the 1280s, was officially appointed. A body which later became the Generalitat was set up to regulate financial and political concerns.

Ferdinand and Isabella greet Christopher Columbus

Spain United

The marriage of Ferdinand of Aragón-Catalonia (Ferrán II to the Catalans) to Isabella of Castile in 1469 joined the two crowns and formed the nucleus of a united Spanish state. Under the Catholic Monarchs Catalonia was incorporated into Castile. The Catholic church's hard-line Inquisition expelled Jews from Spain and the thriving communities in Barcelona and Girona were particularly badly affected.

Columbus' riches?

After Columbus' voyage to the Americas, he was received by the monarchs in Barcelona's Royal Palace. Despite the gesture, Castile, the power centre of Spain, exclusively exploited New World riches, to the exclusion of Barcelona.

During the 16th century, a Golden Age for Spain, the political influence of Catalonia and Barcelona declined even further. The Habsburg grandson of Ferdinand and Isabella was anointed Charles I of Spain in 1516. He inherited the title of Holy Roman Emperor and became Charles V, with Europe-wide duties that gave him little time for Spain. His son, Philip II, moved the capital of the Spanish empire from Toledo to Madrid.

War and Resistance

In 1640, with Spain and France involved in the Thirty Years' War, Catalonia declared itself an independent republic, allied to France. Spanish troops besieged and captured Barcelona in 1651 and after the French defeat in 1659, Catalan territories north of the Pyrenees were ceded to France, fixing the border where it is today. The ensuing years were rife with wars and disputes over succession to the crown, in which Barcelona automatically sided with whoever opposed Madrid.

The worst of these episodes came in the War of the Spanish Succession (1702–13) between the backers of Philip of Anjou, grandson of Louis XIV of France, and the Habsburg claimant, Archduke Charles of Austria. Charles was enthusiastically received when he landed in Catalonia, but Philip, supported by France, won the war and became the first Bourbon ruler, Philip V. After a 13-month siege, on 11 September 1714, the royal army captured and sacked Barcelona. The Catalan Generalitat was dissolved and the city's privileges abolished. The Ciutadella fortress was built to keep the populace subdued, and official use of the Catalan language was outlawed. Catalonia celebrates this date as its national holiday, the Diada, a symbol of the spirit of nationalist resistance.

Discord within the Spanish government or conflict with foreign powers frequently served as an excuse for Catalan separatists to rise up, though their rebellions were usually summarily squashed. From 1808 to 1814, Spain again became a battleground, with British forces opposing Napoleon in the Peninsular War. Napoleon attacked and destroyed Catalonia's sacred shrine, the monastery at Montserrat.

The spirit of European liberalism was late in reaching Spain. After many reverses, a republic, a constitutional monarchy and a democratic constitution were instituted in 1873. Shortly afterwards, Barcelona was at long last given the right to trade with the colonies of the New World.

The maritime empire's glory is showcased in the Museu Marítim

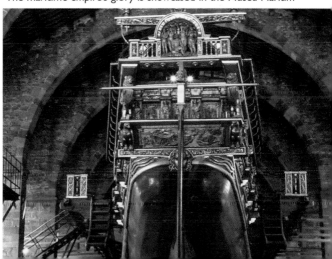

Industrialisation

Meanwhile, the city had gone about its business, devoting its energies to industrialisation. Barcelona's medieval walls were torn down to make way for an expansion in the mid-19th century. The Eixample, an elegant modern district, was laid out on a grid of broad avenues where the new industrialists built mansions. Wealthy patrons supported such architects as Antoni Gaudí and Lluís Domènech i Muntaner. Prosperity was accompanied by a revival in arts and letters, a period known in Catalan as the Renaixença (Renaissance). The city bid for worldwide recognition with the Universal Exposition of 1888, on the site of the Ciutadella fortress.

The Arc de Triomf, built for the 1888 Universal Exposition

With the industrial expansion, an urban working class evolved. Agitation for social justice and regionalist ferment created a combustible atmosphere, and the city became the scene of strikes and anarchist violence. The modern Socialist Party and the UGT, Spain's largest trade union, were founded, and industrialists sought Catalan autonomy as a way to be freed from interference from Madrid. In 1914 a provincial government, the Mancomunitat, was formed, uniting the four Catalan provinces – Barcelona, Tarragona, Lleida, and Girona. It was dissolved in 1923 by

General Primo de Rivera, who established a military dictatorship and banned the Catalan language.

Civil War

In 1931, the Second Republic was established, and King Alfonso XIII escaped to exile. Catalonia won a charter establishing home rule, restoration of the regional parliament and flag,

Montjuïc Exhibition

Despite the Primo de Rivera dictatorship, Barcelona plunged into preparations for another International Exhibition, with monumental buildings and sports facilities on Montjuïc hill, many of which can still be seen today. It opened just before the stock market crash of 1929.

and recognition of Catalan as the official language. Elements in the Spanish army rebelled in 1936, initiating the brutal Civil War. Many churches in Barcelona were put to the torch by anti-clerical mobs. The firmly Republican city was a rallying point for the International Brigade. Barcelona was one of the last cities to fall to the rebel troops of General Francisco Franco at the war's end in 1939.

The Civil War ended with some 700,000 combatants dead; another 30,000 were executed, including many priests and nuns; perhaps as many as 15,000 civilians were killed in air raids and numerous refugees left the country. Catalonia paid a heavy price in defeat. Franco abolished all regional institutions and established central controls. The Catalan language was proscribed, even in schools and churches. For years, Barcelona received little financial support from Madrid, and Spain remained essentially cut off from the rest of Europe.

Recovery

Despite this cultural and political repression and the depressed post-war years, by the 1960s the industrious Catalans were again forging ahead, making this corner of Spain the most successful economically. The traditional textile sector was overtaken by the more prosperous iron, steel and chemical industries, which called for manpower, so people from the less prosperous rural regions of Spain flocked to Barcelona. Sprawling suburbs with ugly high rise buildings mushroomed around the city in an uncontrolled fashion. Franco's government promoted tourism in the 1960s, and crowds from the North began to descend on the Costa Brava. Speculators exploited the coastline but the economy boomed.

The dictatorship ended with Franco's death in 1975. Juan Carlos, grandson of Alfonso XIII, became king and Spain made a rapid and successful transition to democracy. In Catalonia cava flowed in the streets on the day Franco died and the Generalitat was restored as the governing body of the autonomous region. The Catalan language was made official and a renaissance of culture and traditions has followed, seen in literature, theatre, television, films, cultural centres, arts festivals and popular fiestas.

In Barcelona the charismatic Socialist mayor Pasqual Maragall was instrumental in shaping today's modern city by using the '92 Olympics as an excuse to start a radical programme of urban reform to remedy the years of neglect by central government. The momentum of this drive continued after the Olympics and launched Barcelona into the 21st century where it enjoys a newfound status as a top business and conference centre and ranks high amongst European cities for its quality of life.

Catalans are very proud of their flag and their language

ESTAT CATALA

Historical Landmarks

237BC Carthaginian Hamilcar Barca makes base at Barcino.

206BC Romans defeat Carthaginians.

AD531–54 Barcelona capital of Visigoths.

711 Moorish invasion of Spain. They remain there till 1492.

878 Wilfred (Guifré) the Hairy founds dynasty of counts of Barcelona.

1096–1131 Ramón Berenguer III extends Catalan empire.

1213–76 Jaume I consolidates empire, expands Barcelona.

1359 Corts Catalanes (Parliament of Catalonia) established.

1469 Ferdinand and Isabella unite Aragón and Castile.

1494 Administration of Catalonia put under Castilian control.

1516 Carlos I (Charles V, Holy Roman Emperor) takes throne.

1659 Catalan territories north of Pyrenees ceded to France.

1701–13 War of Spanish Succession.

1713–14 Siege of Barcelona by Felipe V's forces; Ciutadella fortress built.

1808–14 Peninsular War between England and France.

1888 Barcelona hosts its first Universal Exposition.

1914 Mancomunitat (provincial government) formed in Catalonia.

1923 General Primo de Rivera sets up dictatorship and bans Catalan.

1931 Republican party comes to power.

1932 Catalonia granted short-lived statute of independence.

1936–9 Civil War ends in Franco's rule and isolates Spain.

1975 Franco dies; Juan Carlos becomes king.

1979 Statute of Autonomy; Catalan restored as official language.

1980 Jordi Pujol becomes president of Catalonia.

1986 Spain joins European Community (European Union). A massive wave of building in Barcelona.

1992 The Olympics are held in Barcelona.

2003 Pujol replaced as president of Catalonia by Pasqual Maragall.

2004 The city extends north, around Diagonal Mar, for Forum 2004.

2006 A new Catalan statute is passed. Jordi Hereu becomes the third socialist mayor of the city. Maragall stands down, replaced by José Montilla as president.

WHERE TO GO

Barcelona can be approached by neighbourhood or by theme. You can set out to see the Gothic Quarter, Montjuïc hill, or the waterfront; or you can create a tour around the works of Gaudí and his fellow modernista architects. It's very tempting to try to sandwich everything into a couple of days, but leave time to get sidetracked in a colourful food market or an alley of antiques shops, or to peek in a quiet courtyard. Take a breather, sit at a pavement café while you linger over a drink, read a newspaper, and watch the people go by.

In the old town, the best way to travel is on foot. Each area – Barri Gòtic, La Ribera, El Raval, La Rambla – and the Eixample district can be covered as a walking tour. For sights further afield, including Montjuïc, Barceloneta and the waterfront, Tibidabo, and two of the top Gaudí attractions, La Sagrada Família and Parc Güell, it's best to make use of Barcelona's excellent public transport network – clean and efficient metro, suburban trains, modern buses, funiculars and cable cars – as well as plenty of inexpensive taxis *(see Public Transport, page 121)*. A good map is essential, but it's easy to be fooled by how close things look on paper.

LA RAMBLA

To call **La Rambla** a street is to do it woeful injustice. Barcelona's most famous boulevard – energetic, artistic, democratic and indulgent – is an intoxicating parade of humanity. You will no doubt want to sample it several times during your stay (maybe even several times a day). It is most crowded just before the (late) lunch hour and in the early

Plaça de Catalunya, the hub of Barcelona

evening on weekdays and at dusk at weekends, though it is never deserted. In the wee hours it's populated by a motley mix of newspaper sellers, street-sweepers and late-night revellers stumbling back to their apartments and hotels.

The broad, tree-shaded, promenade stretches nearly 2km (1 mile) down a gentle incline from the city's hub, Plaça de Catalunya *(see page 52)*, to the waterfront. La Rambla takes its name from an Arabic word meaning a sandy, dry river bed, and it was a shallow gully until the 14th century, when Barcelona families began to construct homes nearby. As the area became more populated, the stream was soon paved over.

Dancing on the Rambla de Canaletes

To the north of La Rambla (left as you walk down it) is the Gothic Quarter; to the south, or right, is El Raval.

Canaletes

The five sections of La Rambla change in character, as they do in name (hence it is often called the 'Ramblas'), as you stroll along. The short **Rambla de Canaletes** at the top, named after the **Font de Canaletes**, the fountain that is one of the symbols of the city, is where crowds pour in from the Plaça de Catalunya or emerge from the metro and railway stations beneath. On Sunday and Monday in football season you'll find noisy knots of fans replaying the games of Barça, Barcelona's beloved club Barcelona FC; if an important match has just been won, look out. Here, too, begin the stalls where you can buy a selection of foreign newspapers and magazines, as well as books, a reflection of Barcelona's status as Spain's publishing centre. You'll also see the first of the ubiquitous human statues, portraying Columbus, a priest, a bearded nun, or a Roman soldier, among numerous guises.

Rambla de les Flors

Birds and Flowers

Next is **Rambla dels Estudis**, popularly called **Rambla dels Ocells** (Rambla of the Birds) because here the boulevard becomes an outdoor aviary where winged creatures of all descriptions are sold. When the vendors leave at the end of the day, their cage-lined stalls are folded and shut like wardrobes, with the birds rustling about inside.

Birds give way to flowers in the **Rambla de les Flors**, officially the **Rambla de Sant Josep**. People flock here on 23 April, the feast day of Sant Jordi (St George), celebrated as Day of the Book because it is also the anniversary of Cervantes' death in 1616. A woman traditionally gives her man a book, and a man gives a woman a rose – both of which are available in abundance along La Rambla. Keep an eye peeled on the right side of the road for the delectable *modernista* pastry and chocolate shop, **Escribà** (Antiga Casa Figueres), its fanciful swirls on the outside a match for the delicacies within.

La Boqueria is the city's most famous market

Facing the Rambla is the elegant **Palau de la Virreina**, a grand palace completed in 1778 for the young widow of the viceroy of colonial Peru. The palace houses a gallery with changing contemporary art exhibits and a branch of the city's Department of Culture where you can find out what is currently happening in the city, and buy tickets for performances and exhibitions. There is a small shop with books and souvenirs.

La Boqueria

On the right-hand side of the street is one of La Rambla's great attractions: the **Mercat de Sant Josep**, usually called **La Boqueria**. This ornate, 19th-century covered market is a cornucopia of delights for the senses: fresh fish, meats, sausages, fruits and vegetables, and all kinds of spices, neatly braided ropes of garlic, sun-dried tomatoes and peppers, preserves and sweetmeats, to make a gourmand swoon. La Boqueria is also a startlingly vibrant community, where shoppers and merchants greet each other by name, ribald sallies across the aisles set off gales of laughter, and the freshness of the *rape* (an angler fish popular in Catalonia) is debated with passion.

The huge market is laid out under high-ceilinged ironwork naves, like a railway station. Restaurants in and near the market are like first-aid stations for those who become faint with hunger. The market opens before dawn and keeps going till early evening. The best time to visit is when practised shoppers and restaurateurs go – early in the morning.

The heart of the Rambla is nearby, at the Pla de la Boqueria, a busy intersection near the Liceu metro station paved with an unmistakable Joan Miró mosaic. Here stands one of Europe's great opera houses, the **Gran Teatre del Liceu** (guided tours daily at 10am, unguided tours daily at 11.30am, noon, 12.30pm and 1pm), inaugurated in 1861. Montserrat Caballé and Josep Carreras made their reputations singing at this theatre, a monument of the Catalan Renaissance and favourite haunt of the Catalan élite. The opera house was gutted by a fire in 1994 (the third it has suffered). After a stunning restoration project that preserved the soul of the historic theatre while adding technological improvements and doubling its size, the Liceu reopened in 1999.

Directly across the Rambla is the Cafè de l'Òpera, a handsome, *modernista*-style café that's always busy and retains a local feel although it is also popular with visitors. It's a good spot for refreshment before you push on down the **Rambla dels Caputxins**. The Rambla's character, like the incline, goes downhill after the Liceu, but the street-entertainment factor rises in inverse proportion. Wade your way through jugglers, human statues, fire-eaters, tarot-card readers, lottery-ticket sellers, hair-braiders and street artists rapidly knocking out portraits, caricatures and chalk masterworks on the pavement.

The Cafè de l'Òpera is a Barcelona institution

Palau Güell

On the right side of the street is the **Hotel Oriente** *(see page 133)*, which preserves a 17th-century Franciscan convent and cloister inside. Note the naïve painted angels floating over the doorway of what was Ernest Hemingway's favourite Barcelona lodging. Just beyond, on Carrer Nou de la Rambla is **Palau Güell** (currently under restoration; due to reopen in 2007), the mansion that Gaudí *(see page 52)* built in 1885 for his principal patron, textile tycoon Count Eusebi Güell. This extraordinary building is structured around an enormous salon, from which a conical roof covered in mosaic tiles emerges to preside over an unusual landscape of capriciously placed battlements, balustrades and strangely shaped chimneys. Although the interior is presently closed to visitors, it's still worth a detour just off the Rambla to take a look at the facade.

On the roof of Palau Güell

Plaça Reial

Returning to the Rambla, cross over and take the short stretch that leads into the arcaded **Plaça Reial**. This handsome, spacious square is graced with a fountain, palm trees, and wrought-iron lampposts designed by the young Gaudí. Like the Boqueria and other landmarks, this square came into being as a result of the destruction of a convent, when church property was expropriated in the mid-19th century. Despite efforts to clean it up, it is still the stomping grounds of junkies and petty thieves, and there is always a police presence, but it is fun, flush with bars, cafés, restaurants, a jazz club and flamenco bar, and buzzing with action night and day.

Stop for a drink and watch the action in the Plaça Reial

Leading down to the harbour is the short **Rambla de Santa Mònica**, beginning at the Plaça del Teatre, site of the Teatre Principal. The Centre d'Art Santa Mònica, in a converted convent, puts on fine contemporary art exhibits. The warren of alleys to the right forms the area once known as the **Barri Xino**. It was once pretty seedy and is still not the best place for a midnight stroll, but some of the old bars are becoming fashionable again, while the atmospheric Pastís bar has not changed in decades.

Carrer dels Escudellers, a busy pedestrian street on the other side of the Rambla, is the gateway to a district of clubs, bars, restaurants and trendy boutiques, and the delights of the Gothic Quarter. At its far end, the recently created Plaça George Orwell has become a trendy place to congregate.

Nearer the port is the **Museu de Cera de Barcelona** (open Mon–Fri 10am–1.30pm and 4–7.30pm, Sat–Sun 11am–2pm and 4.30–8.30pm; daily 10am–10pm in summer), a tourist trap with 300-plus wax effigies. The Rambla ends at the broad, open space facing the **Monument a Colom**, a statue honouring Christopher Columbus that can be climbed for good views of the port. Just beyond lies Barcelona's revitalised waterfront.

The Cathedral

BARRI GÒTIC

From its beginnings more than 2,000 years ago, Barcelona has grown outwards in rings, like concentric ripples on a pond. The ancient core is a hill the Romans called Mont Tàber, where they raised a temple to Augustus Caesar and in the 4th century AD built high walls about 1½km (1mile) long to protect their settlement. This is the nucleus of the medieval district called the **Barri Gòtic**. Although much of it is not really Gothic, it is a remarkable concentration of medieval palaces and churches.

The Cathedral

The best place to begin a tour is the superb **Catedral** (open daily 8am–12.45pm and 5.15–7.30pm), the neighbourhood's focal point. It was begun in 1298 on the site of earlier churches going back to Visigothic times. The final touch – the florid Gothic facade – was not completed until the end of the 19th century and thus contrasts with the simple, octagonal towers. The ribs of the cathedral's high vault are joined at carved and painted keystone medallions, a typically Catalan feature. In the centre of the nave is a splendid Gothic choir with lacy spires. Above are the heraldic emblems of the European kings and princes invited by Charles V to be members of his exclusive Order of the

Golden Fleece. The first and only meeting was held in the cathedral in 1519. The seats reserved for Henry VIII of England and François I of France are next to the emperor's, but they didn't turn up.

Steps under the altar lead to the alabaster tomb of Santa Eulàlia, one of the city's two patron saints, martyred in the 4th century. On the wall of the right aisle are the tombs of Count Ramón Berenguer I and his wife Almodis, who founded the earlier cathedral on this spot in 1058. Don't miss the Catalan Gothic altarpieces in the chapels behind the altar; the nine panels of the Transfiguration painted for the Sant Salvador chapel in the 15th century by Bernat Martorell are considered his masterpiece.

The leafy cloister is a lively refuge, with birds fluttering among the orange, magnolia and palm trees and inhabited by 13 geese, symbolising the age of Eulàlia when she died. Watch where you walk, as the cloister is paved with tombstones, badly worn, but many still bearing the ancient emblems of the bootmakers', tailors' and other craft guilds whose wealth helped pay for the cathedral. From the cloister, pass to the **Capella de Santa Llúcia**, a chapel with 13th- and 14th-century tombstones on the floor and a monument to a crusader knight in armour on one wall.

Shaded spot in the Barri Gòtic

Leaving the chapel by its front entrance, turn left into Carrer del Bisbe. Look up as you walk through the old town to take in the details – a curious hanging sign, a lantern, an unusual sculpture or plants trailing from balconies. On the right is a row of gargoyles leaning from the roof of the Palau de la Generalitat, where there is also a richly ornamented gateway. The lacy overhead bridge is Gothic in style but is actually a 1929 addition.

Plaça Sant Jaume

Just ahead is the **Plaça Sant Jaume**, the heart of the Barri Gòtic, where the Government of Catalonia, the Generalitat, faces the Casa de la Ciutat (city hall, also known as the Ajuntament). Though the institutions they house are not always in agreement, the two buildings are a harmonious pair: both have classical facades that hide their Gothic origins. To visit either building, you'll need luck or planning; they can only be visited on certain public holidays, such as 23 April (Sant Jordi, patron saint of Catalonia), or at weekends by appointment, though concerts are held in the Casa de la Ciutat from time to time.

Palau de la Generalitat, the seat of Catalan government

The **Palau de la Generalitat**, located on the north side of the square (the one closer to the Cathedral), is the more interesting of the two. It dates from 1359, when it was made the executive branch, reporting to the Corts Catalanes. The nucleus of the present building is the main patio – pure

Catalan Gothic, with an open staircase leading to a gallery of arches on slender pillars. The star feature here is the flamboyant Gothic facade of the **Capella de Sant Jordi**. The **Saló de Sant Jordi** (there's no escaping St George), a vaulted hall in the 17th-century front block of the building, is lined with modern murals of historical scenes.

High and mighty

The Plaça Sant Jaume is the meeting place for the giants *(gegants)*, the huge regal figures that process through the streets at the festival of La Mercè, the city's patron, in September. It is also where you will see *castells* – human towers reaching nine people high – an attraction at various fiestas.

The **Ajuntament**, or Casa de la Ciutat, across the plaza, has held Barcelona's city hall since 1372. It was here that the Consell de Cent, a council of 100 notable citizens, met to deal with civic affairs under the watchful eyes of the king. The original entrance can be seen around the left corner of the building, on the Carrer de la Ciutat. Inside, the left staircase leads to the upper gallery of the old courtyard and to the **Saló de Cent** (Hall of the One Hundred) with a barrel-vaulted ceiling. The red-and-yellow bars of Catalonia's flag decorate the walls. The hall where the city council now meets adjoins, and at the head of the black marble staircase is the **Saló de les Cròniques** (Hall of the Chronicles), noted for the modern murals in sepia tones by Josep Maria Sert.

From behind the Ajuntament, take the short Carrer d'Hèrcules to Plaça Sant Just for a peek at the church of **Sants Just i Pastor** and the pretty little square on which it sits, evocative of a bygone Barcelona. The church is one of the oldest in the city, though it was repeatedly remodelled. It is said that any will sworn before its altar is recognised as valid by the courts of Barcelona, a practice dating from the 10th century.

Plaça del Rei

Heading back to Plaça Sant Jaume, turn right into Carrer de la Llibreteria, a small street of pastry shops, boutiques and one of Barcelona's oldest and tiniest coffee shops, El Mesón del Café. Two blocks down on the left, on **Plaça del Rei** is the **Museu d'Història de la Ciutat** (City History Museum; open Tues–Sat 10am–2pm, 4–8pm, all day in summer, Sun 10am–3pm). The building is a Gothic mansion that was moved stone by stone to this location. In the basement, excavations have uncovered a portion of the Roman city, including shops running along the inside of the Roman wall.

A stern Renaissance tower dominates Plaça del Rei

Dyeing vats for a clothing industry and evidence of wine-making have been unearthed. Most importantly, however, evidence has been revealed of an early church on the site with a bishop's residence, which provides the link between the Roman and medieval cities.

Above them is the **Palau Reial** (Royal Palace) into which you emerge at the end of the excavations. The main buildings here are the chapel, great hall and tower. The **Capella de Santa Àgata** (Chapel of St Agatha) is notable for the 15th-century altarpiece of the *Adoration of the Magi* by one of Catalonia's finest artists, Jaume Huguet. From a small door in the south side of the church, stone steps lead up beside the great hall into the many-arched Renaissance tower of **Rei Martí** (Martin the Humanist, last of the dynasty of Barcelona counts) that dominates Plaça del Rei.

The cool courtyard of the Museu Frederic Marès

The vast, barrel-vaulted great hall or throne room, the **Saló del Tinell**, was built for royal audiences in 1359 under Pere III (the Ceremonius) by Guillem Carbonell. On occasion the Corts Catalanes (Parliament) met here. This is where Ferdinand and Isabella received Columbus in 1493 on his return from his first voyage to the Americas. It was later used as a church, and by the Inquisition, whose victims were burned at the stake in the square. Concerts are sometimes held in the Tinell, and theatre and concert performances are held in the square in summer.

Behind the Royal Palace, off Carrer Tapineria, is Plaça de Berenguer el Gran, which has a well-preserved section of the original Roman wall. The defences were 9m (30ft) high, 3.5m (12ft) thick and marked at intervals by towers 18m (59ft) tall. Until 1943, most of this section was covered by old houses, which were removed to restore the walls to view.

Towards the Museu Frederic Marès

A former wing of the palace which encloses the Plaça del Rei was rebuilt in 1557 to become the **Palau del Lloctinent** (Palace of the Lieutenant), residence of the king's representative. The entrance, reached by leaving the square and turning right on the Carrer dels Comtes, is an elegant patio with a noble staircase and remarkable carved wooden ceiling.

Just beyond, flanking the cathedral, is the **Museu Frederic Marès** (open Tues–Sat 10am–7pm, Sun 10am–3pm), which has a beautiful courtyard. Marès, a 20th-century sculptor of civic statues, was a compulsive collector who bequeathed to Barcelona an unusually idiosyncratic collection of art and miscellany. The lower floors of the museum are stocked with Iberian votive figurines, Limoges enamel boxes and religious sculptures. You'll also find Portuguese carved ox yokes, a roomful of iron keys, old sewing machines, canes, wind-up toys – in short, an endless catalogue of art and artefacts. There is even the suitcase, covered with travel stickers, which Marès used to cart home his loot.

Roman Remains and the Jewish Ghetto

Retracing your steps on the narrow street flanking the cathedral, circle around to the rear and duck into the narrow

The Call

Barcelona's Jews, though noted as doctors, scholars and jewellers, were confined to the Call and forced to wear long, hooded cloaks with yellow headbands. Taxation of the community was a source of royal income. This did not save the Call from being burned and looted as persecution of the Jews throughout Spain mounted in the 13th and 14th centuries. Eventually the Jews of Barcelona were killed, expelled or forcibly converted to Christianity, and their synagogues were turned into churches. Just off Carrer del Call, at Carrer de Marlet 1, a medieval inscription in Hebrew marks the site of a hospital founded by one 'Rabbi Samuel Hassareri, may his life never cease'. In the same street part of a synagogue has been revealed.

Carrer del Paradís. Here, just inside the doorway of the Centre Excursionista de Catalunya, four columns of the Roman Temple of Augustus are embedded in the wall.

Menorah in the Sinagoga Major

Since ancient times, when two main Roman thoroughfares intersected at the Plaça Sant Jaume, this has been the crossroads of Barcelona. Streets radiate in all directions, each an invitation to explore the Barri Gòtic. The **Carrer del Call** leads into the labyrinth of narrow streets that was the Call, or Jewish Quarter, until the late 14th century. Today the quarter bustles with antiques shops and dealers of rare books, plus bars and restaurants frequented by antiquarians and artists. At No. 5 Carrer Marlet part of a former synagogue, **Sinagoga Major**, has been opened up and can be visited.

Nearby is the little street called Baixada de Santa Eulàlia and just off it is **Plaça de Sant Felip Neri**, a tiny and silent square closed to traffic (silent except when children from the nearby school come out to play here). The saint's church was pockmarked by Italian bombs during the Civil War, though some maintain that firing squads performed executions here.

Antique Alley

The Baixada de Santa Eulàlia descends to **Carrer dels Banys Nous**, named for the long-gone 12th-century 'new' baths of the ghetto. This winding street, which more or less follows the line of the old Roman wall, is the unofficial boundary of the Barri Gòtic. It is also known as the Carrer dels Antiquaris

Inside Santa Maria del Pi

– the street of antiques dealers. Keep your eyes peeled for unusual hand-painted shop signs, the fretwork of Gothic balconies, and dusty treasures in the shop windows. You will also notice the old tile signs with a cart symbol high on the walls, the indication of one-way streets.

A Trio of Plazas

Around the corner is a trio of impossibly pretty plazas. **Plaça Sant Josep Oriol** adjoins **Plaça del Pi**, on which sits **Santa Maria del Pi**, a handsome church with a tall, octagonal bell tower and a harmonious facade pierced by a large 15th-century rose window. 'Pi' means pine tree, and there is a small one here replacing the landmark specimen of past centuries. Buildings in the plaça show the sgrafitto technique of scraping designs in coloured plaster, imported from Italy in the early 1700s. Barcelona's emerging merchant class favoured such facades as an inexpensive substitute for the sculptures on aristocratic palaces.

These adjoining squares, together with the smaller **Placeta del Pi** to the rear of the church, are the essence of old Barcelona and a great place to while away the hours. The bars with tables spread out under leafy trees in each of the squares are magnets for young people and travellers, who are entertained by roving musicians. On Sunday, artists offer their canvases for sale in lively Plaça Sant Josep Oriol, where the Bar del Pi is a popular meeting place. On Saturday and Sunday, dairy produce and honey are sold from stalls.

The street that leads north from Plaça del Pi, **Carrer Petritxol**, is one of the Barri Gòtic's most traditional. The narrow alley is lined with art galleries, framing shops and traditional *granjas* – good stops for pastries and hot chocolate. Barcelona's oldest and most famous art gallery is **Sala Parés** at No. 5.

Around Plaça Nova

At Carrer Portaferrisa, a left turn will take you to La Rambla, while a right turn will take you back to the cathedral and a handful of additional sights on the perimeter of the Barri Gòtic. (You could also return to Plaça Sant Josep Oriol and take Carrer de la Palla.) Back at **Plaça Nova**, in front of the cathedral, is the modern Col.legi d'Arquitectes (College of Architects). Picasso designed the graffiti-like drawings of the Three Kings and children bearing palm branches that are etched on the 1960s facade. For three weeks in December, a market selling Nativity figures and christmas trees occupies the Plaça Nova – a square that got its name, 'New', in 1356 and has held markets for nearly 1,000 years. Look for the strange, quintessential Catalan figure, *el caganer* – the red-capped peasant squatting and defecating beside the manger.

The pedestrian thoroughfare that leads north to Plaça de Catalunya is **Avda**

The popular Hotel Jardí in the pretty Plaça del Pi

Portal de l'Àngel, one of the city's main shopping streets, especially busy when *rebaixes* (sales) are on. Look for little Carrer Montsió, which leads to **Els Quatre Gats** (The Four Cats), a bar and restaurant that became famous when Picasso and a group of young intellectuals – painters Ramón Casas and Santiago Rusiñol among them – frequented it. Picasso had his first exhibition here in 1901, and the bar, one of the first commissions for the *modernista* architect Puig i Cadafalch, preserves its turn-of-the-20th-century ambience and is, understandably, a great favourite with visitors to Barcelona.

Majestic Santa Maria del Mar has wonderful acoustics

LA RIBERA

Some of the most beautiful Gothic architecture and most fascinating medieval corners of Barcelona lie just outside the Barri Gòtic. To the east of Via Laietana – a traffic-filled avenue roughly parallel to the Ramblas, which was cut through the city in 1859 to link the port with the modern centre – and below the Carrer de la Princesa, which intersects it at midpoint, is the atmospheric quarter called **La Ribera**. Here you'll find both the Museu Picasso and the majestic church of **Santa Maria del Mar** (open 9am–1.30pm, 4.30–8pm). Carrer

Argenteria cuts a diagonal swathe from Plaça de l'Angel to the church. Begun in 1329 at the height of Catalonia's expansion as a Mediterranean power, it is the greatest example of pure Catalan Gothic, with unadorned exterior walls, a sober facade flanked by three-tiered octagonal bell towers, and a beautiful rose window over the portal.

A quiet corner in El Born

The dimensions and austerity of the interior are breathtaking. Fires during Civil War rioting in 1936 consumed all the trappings of chapels, choir and altar, leaving the interior stripped to its essence. The result is a lofty hall suffused with soft light from the stained-glass windows. Three naves are supported by slim, octagonal columns set 13m (43ft) apart, and the dimensions of the interior are multiples of this distance, achieving a perfect symmetry. Behind the simple altar, the columns branch high overhead into the arched vaulting of the apse.

The acoustics are excellent, best demonstrated by the concerts held in the church and the voices of choirboys at Mass. Santa Maria is much favoured for weddings so you may find it closed to the public if one is in progress when you arrive.

El Born

The rear door of the church leads to the **Passeig del Born**, a pretty, rectangular plaza where jousts were held in the Middle Ages and which today is full of smart galleries, restaurants, bars and chic shops – very much the place to be, especially for the young. Many of the little streets surrounding the church are named after the craftsmen who once worked here, such as Sombrerers (Hatmakers), Mirallers (Mirror-makers) and Espasería (Sword-makers). The area is better known now for the people who fill its designer bars late into the night and spill out onto the streets; disgruntled residents hang signs from their windows pleading with the municipal government to impose 'quiet hours'. At the end, the magnificent, wrought-iron **Mercat del Born**, the old fruit-and-vegetable market, is being converted into a cultural centre.

Carrer Montcada and the Museu Picasso

One of Barcelona's grandest medieval streets, **Carrer Montcada**, populated by aristocrats from the 14th to the 16th centuries, is lined with splendid Gothic palaces, each with an imposing door or arched gate to an inner courtyard from where an ornamental staircase usually led up to reception rooms. These mansions were gradually abandoned after the demolition of the adjoining district and construction of the

Pablo Picasso

The world's most acclaimed 20th-century artist, Pablo Ruiz y Picasso was born in 1881 in Málaga, the son of an art teacher, whose work took the family to Barcelona. Pablo began his art studies here and became part of a group of innovative artists and writers. In 1900, Picasso first visited Paris, and settled there four years later. He never returned to Barcelona after 1934 and, had he wanted to do so, his opposition to the Franco regime would have made it impossible, but his work always retained strong Spanish links. When Picasso died in 1973 (two years before the death of Franco and the end of the dictatorship), the bulk of his own collection, now in the Musée Picasso in Paris, went to the French government in a deal to settle taxes.

Ciutadella fortress. This quarter is the most authentically medieval part of the city.

The **Museu Picasso** (open Tues–Sun 10am–8pm), occupies five palaces (two used for temporary exhibitions). The main entrance is through the 15th-century **Palau Aguilar**. The buildings were acquired by the city to house the collection of paintings, drawings and ceramics donated by Picasso's lifelong friend and secretary, Jaume Sabartés. After the museum opened in 1963, Picasso added sketches and paintings from his childhood and youth. The earliest works date from his ninth year. As a teenager he produced large canvases in the

The youthful Picasso, as depicted by his friend, Ramón Casas

19th-century realist style, such as the *First Communion* and *Science and Charity*. It appears that, as Picasso's talent developed, he digested the styles of the past and of his contemporaries, proved he could equal them, then forged ahead.

The collection of his work is the largest outside Paris, and while it doesn't possess any of his finest pieces, it does have two good examples of his Blue Period (1901–4), as well as *The Harlequin* (1917), and the idiosyncratic *Las Meninas* series, the variations on the theme of the Velázquez masterpiece in Madrid's Prado Museum, which provides a fascinating view of Picasso's innovative and deconstructivist approach to his subject.

More Mansions and Museums

Across the street is the **Museu Tèxtil i de la Indumentària** (Textile and Costume Museum; open Tues–Sat 10am–6pm, Sun 10am–3pm), in the former palace of the Marqueses de Lió. The collection brings to life the elegance enjoyed by the wealthy families who occupied the Montcada mansions. The costumes on display are of superb silks, satins and furs, embroidered and stitched to perfection. Styles represented reach all the way to the flapper dresses of the 1920s. There is a delightful café and an interesting shop in its atmospheric courtyard.

Situated within a 16th-century palace the **Museu Barbier-Mueller d'Art Precolombí**, (Montcada 14; open Tues–Fri 11am–7pm, Sat 10am–7pm, Sun 10am–3pm) showcases a collection of pre-Columbian art. All the mansions along here merit a peek in at the courtyards, but one that's always open is the handsome, baroque **Palau Dalmases** (No. 20). On the ground floor is an over-the-top, rococo bar, Espai Barroc (Baroque Space). At the end of the street, in Plaçeta Montcada, you can get wonderful Basque tapas in the Euskaletxea bar.

Montcada mansion

Palau de la Música

Up Via Laietana several blocks from Carrer Princesa, at Sant Francesc de Paula 2, is one of the city's greatest achievements of *modernista*

▶ architecture, the **Palau de la Música Catalana** (guided tours daily 10am–3.30pm). Designed by Lluís Domènech i Montaner, it is the perfect expression of *modernisme*, and has been designated a UNESCO World Heritage Site. It is an explosion of mosaics, tiles, stained glass, enamel, sculpture and carving – a wildly audacious outpouring of contours and colours. The brick exterior, with Moorish

The original ticket booth at the Palau de la Música Catalana

arches and columns inlaid with floral tiles, is sober compared to what's inside, where every square inch is embellished.

One of Domènech's main concerns was to let in as much natural light as possible, and the hall is light and roomy. The structural skeleton is iron – an innovation in those days – which allows the walls to be made of glass. Sunlight streaming in during afternoon concerts sets the place on fire. On either side of the stage the rich colours of the room are offset by sculpted groups of musical masters in white plaster. Between them, the silvery pipes of a grand organ stand in orderly contrast. A curved wall is covered with mosaics of muses playing instruments; their upper bodies are made of porcelain and seem to emerge magically from the walls. Overhead is the Palau's crowning glory, a magical, stained-glass orb.

The best way to experience the Palau is to attend a concert. Programmes range from classical recitals to jazz (box office open 10am–9pm; tel: 902 442 882, <www.palau musica.org>). The alleyways opposite lead to Santa Caterina market, a dazzling renovation by architects EMBT, creators of the Scottish Parliament building, and a great place to eat.

Discordant roofs on the Illa de la Discòrdia

EL EIXAMPLE

The **Eixample**, north of Plaça de Catalunya, is the city's main shopping and commercial area. You will probably want to spend a lot of time here if you are interested in Gaudí. The neighbourhood has spectacular apartment blocks, examples of early 20th-century *modernista* architecture, and the central part is known as the **Quadrat d'Or** (Golden Square).

The principal avenues are the elegant Passeig de Gràcia, Barcelona's version of the Champs d'Elysee, and the Rambla de Catalunya. In a manageable area between the Gran Vía de les Corts Catalanes and Avinguda Diagonal, you'll find most of the *modernista* masterpieces. Two of Barcelona's signature sights, Gaudí's unfinished cathedral La Sagrada Família and his fantasy-land Parc Güell *(see pages 53–56)*, are on the northern outskirts of the Eixample (easily accessible by taxi or metro, and the former on foot).

Despite the exuberance of the architecture, the city's modern district is a model of rationalist urban planning, a rigid geometric grid simply called 'the Extension'. The outrageous and conservative coexist here without much fuss. Barcelona's expansion came about in a remarkable burst of urban development. By the mid-1800s the city was bursting at the seams and suffocating inside its ring of medieval walls. A competition was held in 1859 to select a plan for a new quarter between the old city and the Collserola hills. The job went to an engineer named Ildefons Cerdà, whose plan quintupled the city's size in a matter of decades. The Eixample construction transformed Barcelona into a showcase of extravagant *modernista* architecture, and the swanky Passeig de Gràcia became the place to be seen. Barcelona used the 1888 Universal Exposition as an open house to show the world its new face.

The Illa de la Discòrdia

The best place to begin a *modernista* tour is on Passeig de Gràcia, with its single, hallucinatory block popularly known as the **Illa de la Discòrdia** (Block of Discord), set between Consell de Cent and Aragó. It gained its name because of the three stunning buildings in markedly different architectural styles that are located almost next door to each other.

At No. 35 Domènech i Montaner's impressive **Casa Lleó Morera** (1902–6) incorporates both Moorish and Gothic elements. This grand apartment house has suffered some disfigurement, especially on the ground floor, where the Spanish leather goods company Loewe installed picture windows and destroyed several original sculptures. The building now contains offices and sadly cannot be visited.

At No. 41 is the **Casa Amatller** (1900), which was built for a chocolate manufacturer. Puig i Cadafalch drew inspiration from Flanders for the stepped roof covered in glazed tiles. The Institut Amatller d'Art Hispànic on the top floor contains doc-

The sinuous curved windows of Gaudí's Casa Batlló

uments on Hispanic art and furniture by Puig i Cadafalch. There is an antique elevator and a wonderful staircase in the entrance hall which can be visited.

Casa Batlló

Gaudí's highly personal **Casa Batlló** (1904–6) is next door and can now be visited, to the delight of many (open daily 9am–8pm). The curvy contours, unexpected combinations of textures and materials, bright colours and infinite detail are Gaudí hallmarks, as are his prevalent religious and nationalist symbolism. Casa Batlló is said to pay tribute to the patron saint of Catalonia, Sant Jordi, and the dragon he slayed. Gaudí himself left no clues as to his intent. The undulating blue-tile roof certainly looks like a dragon's scaly hide, while the balconies could be the skulls and bones of its victims (others have suggested they are Venetian carnival masks). Sant Jordi's cross and a shaft suggest a spear being thrust into the dragon's back. Casa Batlló's facade is covered with scraps of broken plate and tile, a decorative technique called *trencadís* that Gaudí employed repeatedly. He did not build the entire house, but remodelled both exterior and interior in 1906.

La Pedrera

Further up and across the street, at No. 92, is **Casa Milà** (open daily Nov–Feb 9am–6.30pm, Mar–Oct 9am–8pm; tel: 902 400 973), Gaudí's masterwork. Known as **La Pedrera** (the Stone Quarry, an allusion to its rippling, limestone surface), this stunning apartment house, built between 1905 and 1910, is a UNESCO World Heritage Site. The sinuous facade, with wonderfully twisted wrought-iron balconies, bends around the corner of Carrer Provença. The building was given a facelift in the mid-1990s, and it looks better than ever. The apartments inside had suffered unspeakable horrors, and Gaudí's beautiful arched attics were sealed up, but today everything has been restored to its original state.

The attic floor is now a handsome, high-tech museum (Espai Gaudí) with an interesting exhibition of his work. One of the original apartments, all odd shapes, hand-crafted door knobs, and idiosyncratic details, has been outfitted with period furniture, many of the pieces designed by Gaudí himself.

La Pedrera had one of the world's first underground parking garages; today the space houses an ampitheatre where cultural conferences are held. The building's owner, the cul-

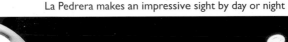

La Pedrera makes an impressive sight by day or night

tural Fundació Caixa de Catalunya, has transformed the second floor into a sumptuous exhibition space for a variety of impressively curated shows.

On summer weekend evenings you can enjoy cocktails and jazz on the terrace. For many, though, the highlight is the wavy rooftop, with its cluster of swirling Darth Vader-like chimneys, known as 'witch scarers' and decorated with recycled tiles, and spectacular views of Barcelona.

The rooftop and chimneys of La Pedrera, bathed in sunlight

More Modernisme

You are likely to be busy looking up or gazing in chic store windows along **Passeig de Gràcia**, but be sure to notice the ground as well: Gaudí designed the hexagonal pavement tiles with nature motifs. The mosaic benches and iron street lamps with little bat motifs (1900) are by Pere Falqués.

Additional examples of *modernisme* are littered throughout the Eixample and are too numerous to detail here. However, details of a special route, the Ruta del Modernisme, which visits 115 examples, can be found in the main tourist office below Plaça Catalunya. A guidebook is also available that gives discounts on entrance tickets.

Have a look at the streets to the east of Passeig de Gràcia, especially Diputació, Consell de Cent, Mallorca and València. In the old town you'll stumble across marvellous *modernista* store fronts, such as the stamp shop at Carrer dels Boters, the Antiga Casa Figueras pastry shop on the Ramblas and the wonderful dining room of the Hotel España in Carrer Sant Pau.

If Barcelona's given you the design bug, the excellent shop **Vinçon**, at Passeig de Gràcia 96, specialises in design. It's well worth a visit, for its inspiring contents as well as for the spectacular turn-of-the-20th-century palace it is housed in. You can explore the mansion that once belonged to Picasso's contemporary, the painter Ramón Casas, whilst finding out how design conscious Barceloneses decorate their homes.

In addition to the jewels of *modernista* architecture, Passeig de Gràcia is lined with cafés, cinemas, galleries, bookstores and elegant fashion boutiques. This is definitely the place for designer shopping, as well as more down-to-earth fashion, such as that at Zara, the Spanish enterprise that has now become internationally known for inexpensive, young

Modernisme

Modernisme, a movement related to the design styles in vogue in Europe in the late 19th century – French Art Nouveau, German and Austrian Jugendstil – was a rebellion against the rigid forms and colourless stone and plaster of classical architecture. In Barcelona the new style assumed nationalist motifs and significance, which may be why it has been so carefully preserved here. Although there was an entire school of *modernista* architects working in Barcelona from the late 19th century until the 1930s, it is customary to speak of the 'Big Three': Antoni Gaudí, who left such a personal mark on the city; Lluís Domènech i Montaner (Palau de la Música Catalana and Casa Morera); and Josep Puig i Cadafalch (Casa Amatller, Casa Terrades and Els Quatre Gats), all of which are described in this guide.

fashion. A number of the city's top hotels are located on or near the Passeig de Gràcia.

Around the Avenues

The **Plaça de Catalunya**, where the boulevard begins, was designed to be the city's hub, and it is certainly a lively cross-roads and meeting place, especially the legendary Café Zurich. The bus, metro, and the regional and national rail systems radiate from this square *(see Public Transport, page 121)* and El Corte Inglés department store occupies the whole of the northern side.

Parallel to Passeig de Gràcia is the Rambla de Catalunya, an extension of the Old Town Ramblas, lined with smart shops, terrace cafés, restaurants and galleries. Traffic moves down either side, but the centre is pedestrian-only and is considerably more sedate than the lower Ramblas.

On Carrer d'Aragó (between Passeig de Gràcia and Rambla Catalunya) is the **Fundació Antoni Tàpies** (open

---

Antoni Gaudí

Count Eusebi Güell, a textile manufacturer, was Gaudí's patient and daring patron, a man who was able to accept the architect's wildly imaginative ideas. The Palau Güell, which Gaudí began in 1885 *(see page 28)*, previews many aspects of his work. Gaudí died in 1926 at the age of 74, and is buried in the crypt of his great cathedral.

He was a deeply pious and conservative man, despite his innovations, and during his last years he lived in a room on the site, obsessed with the project. When passers-by discovered the architect run over by a tram in a nearby street in 1926 and took him to hospital, the doctors, unable at first to identify him, thought the dishevelled old man was a tramp. When it was discovered who he was, the entire city turned out for his funeral.

Tues–Sun 10am–8pm), dedicated to the work of the foremost living artist in Catalonia – and the whole of Spain. In addition to Tàpies' own work, it holds excellent temporary exhibitions, and it is all housed in a gorgeous 1880 Domènech i Montaner building – one of the first examples of *modernisme*. From the outside, viewed from across the street, you can appreciate Tàpies' whimsical, tangled wire sculpture *Núvol i Cadira* (Cloud and Chair) on the roof.

The towers and cranes of
La Sagrada Família

La Sagrada Família

What the Eiffel Tower is to Paris or the Statue of Liberty is to New York, the soaring spires of the **Sagrada Família** (open Apr–Sept daily 9am–8pm, Oct–Mar 9am–6pm) are to Barcelona. Its unmistakable profile, protruding from the city's skyline, is visible from afar. Yet the eight peculiar, cigar-shaped towers are merely the shell of a church that is still many years from completion. This was Antoni Gaudí's life work, though he didn't really expect to finish it in his lifetime. Gaudí took over traditional, neo-Gothic plans of an earlier architect in 1883 and supervised work on the eastern, Nacimiento facade, one tower, and part of the apse and nave. This facade seems to be the one most faithful to Gaudí's intentions.

Everything has significance and no space is left unfilled. The three doorways, with stonework dripping like stalactites, represent Faith, Hope and Charity, and are loaded with sculptures depicting angel choirs, musicians and Biblical episodes such as the birth of Jesus, the Flight into Egypt, the Slaughter of the Innocents, the Tree of Calvary, and much more. Twelve towers, four at each portal, represent the Apostles; four higher ones, the Evangelists; a dome over the apse represents the Virgin; and the central spire the Saviour.

For many years, the church remained much as it was when Gaudí died, but work has been going on since the 1950s – not an easy task, since Gaudí left few plans behind. You can ascend one of the towers (by lift or spiral staircase) for an overview. The western Pasión facade (on Carrer de Sardenya) and its towers have been under construction since 1952, although the sculptures by Josep Maria Subirachs are not to everyone's taste. The work of Japanese sculptor Etsuro Sotoo on the Nacimiento facade is more in keeping with the spirit of Gaudí.

Many people believe the temple should have been left as it was, unfinished, as a tribute to the great Gaudí, but onward it goes, the work supervised by Jordi Bonet Armengol, the son of one of Gaudí's aides. Completion has now finally been set for 2026, one hundred years after Gaudí's death. Until then, the great spires are marred by ever-present scaffolding and cranes that seem almost to have become part of the cathedral.

Parc Güell

A short walk from the Sagrada Família, along Avinguda de Gaudí, is the **Hospital de la Santa Creu i Sant Pau**, designed by Domènech i Montaner. The complex, still a hospital, is one of *modernisme*'s most underrated and least-known works. Visitors can wander through the grounds and admire the structures from outside.

A ceramic encrusted sculpture in Parc Güell

Further north, in a working-class neighbourhood on the hills behind Gràcia, **Parc Güell** (open daily, May–Sept 10am–9pm, Mar–Apr and Oct 10am–7pm, Nov–Feb 10am–6pm), another wildly ambitious Gaudí project, was planned as a residential community, to be intertwined with nature. Gaudí's patron Eusebi Güell bought 6 hectares (15 acres) here, overlooking the city and the sea, intending to create a community of villas. He gave Gaudí carte blanche to produce something original, and for the next 14 years, on and off, the architect let his imagination run wild; much of the design was, however, eventually by Josep Maria Jujol.

Two gingerbread pavilions guard the entrance on Carrer d'Olot, the one on the left is a shop, that on the right an exhibition centre. In front of them is a tiled lizard fountain; supporting columns mimic tree trunks. Ceilings are decorated with fragments of plates, and undulating benches are splashed with colourful ceramic pieces, known as *trencadís*. Beneath the plaza with the benches is the **Saló de les Cent Columnes** (Hall of the One Hundred Columns). There actually are 86, Doric in style, in what was to be the colony's covered market. Dolls' heads, bottles, glasses and plates are stuck in the ceiling mosaics. Only five buildings were completed. Gaudí lived for many years in one, now the **Casa-Museu Gaudí**, a museum of his furniture and memorabilia.

THE WATERFRONT

Barcelona turned its back on the sea during the 19th century and focused on developing industry. The sea wall where families loved to walk and catch the breeze on stifling summer nights was dismantled. Access to the sea was obstructed by warehouses and railway tracks and expansion proceeded towards the hills. Barceloneta, a neighbourhood created in the early 18th century between the port and the beach as part of a military initiative, remained a close-knit working-class community. However, things changed with the creation of an ambitious recreational and commercial area along the waterfront in the early 90s.

The Swallows

A perennial waterfront attraction are the ferries called Golondrinas (Swallows), moored opposite the Columbus Monument. These boats have been taking passengers round the harbour ever since the 1888 World Exposition.

Maritime Heritage

Begin a tour of the waterfront at the Columbus Monument, at the foot of the Ramblas. To the right is **Les Reials Drassanes**, begun in 1255, and now housing the **Museu Marítim** (open daily 10am–8pm). The 16 bays of these great shipyards, which

Port Vell

handled more than 30 galleys, launched ships that extended Catalonia's dominion over the Mediterranean from Tunis to Greece, Sicily, Sardinia and much of the French coast. The museum contains models from the earliest galleys to the cargo and passenger vessels that have made Barcelona their home port. The prize exhibit is a full-size copy of *La Galera Reial*, aboard which Don Juan of Austria commanded the fleet that defeated the Turks at the Battle of Lepanto (1571). A restored early 20th-century cargo vessel, *Santa Eulàlia*, sits in the harbour and can be visited.

Port Vell

At the other side of the busy Passeig de Colom is an undulating wooden walkway and footbridge called the **Rambla del Mar** which stretches across the mouth of the **Port Vell**. It crosses over to the Moll d'Espanya and **Maremàgnum**, a commercial centre with an Imax cinema, lots of shops (open daily until 11pm), bars, discos and restaurants – most serving fast food, but some with terraces which are a great place to sit and watch the harbour activity. Families head for **L'Aquàrium** (open daily 9.30am–9pm in winter, till 11pm in summer); one of Europe's largest aquariums, it has a spectacular glass tunnel running through its huge Oceanarium.

The port is busy with yachts, cruise ships and ferries to Mallorca. Overhead, cable cars link Montjuïc with the Torre de Jaume I and the Torre de Sant Sebastià in Barceloneta. The **World Trade Center**, a complex of offices designed by I.M. Pei, appears to be floating in the harbour.

On the mainland, the **Moll de la Fusta**, the old wood-loading quay, was transformed into a broad promenade in the 1980s, planted with palms and lined with restaurants and clubs. The project proved unsuccessful, however, due to the noise and fumes from the traffic-filled waterfront highway, and it has now been redesigned and landscaped. Where the Moll d'Espanya joins the promenade stands Roy Lichtenstein's colourful Pop Art sculpture, called the **Barcelona Head**.

Heading east, you reach **Marina Port Vell**, a harbour for luxury yachts and chic motor cruisers. On the **Moll de Barceloneta**, in a renovated warehouse complex, the Palau de Mar houses the **Museu d'Història de Catalunya** (open Tues–Sat 10am–7pm, Wed until 8pm, Sun 10am–2.30pm, extended opening times in summer), which is fun as well as informative. Along the Passeig Joan de Borbó parallelling the quay, numerous popular restaurants have outside tables.

Lichtenstein's Barcelona Head

BARCELONETA

If you want to eat really good fish, go to Barceloneta, an area for many years separated from the city in spirit as well as by physical barriers of water and rail yards. It was built in the early 18th century to house dispossessed families when La Ribera district was demolished to make way for the Ciutadella fortress. A robust *barrio* inhabited by fishermen's families, its beaches were scruffy and dominated by flimsy wooden restaurant shacks *(chiringuitos)*.

Eating outdoors in the sunshine in Port Olímpic

When the area was virtually rebuilt in preparation for the 1992 Olympics, they were wiped out, and many Barceloneses nostalgically mourn their loss. You can cut through the grid of narrow streets or walk along the beach to the **Passeig Marítim** and the landscaped promenade running alongside the wooden walkways and scrupulously clean sands of **Platja Barceloneta**. Several modern *chiringuitos* and some good restaurants have now opened on the beach, a popular hangout on summer nights.

Olympic Village

Keep walking and you will come to the 1992 Olympic Village, the **Vila Olímpica**, an award-winning development that has blossomed into a smart and vibrant neighbourhood for

The more beaches they build, the more people fill them

young families and professionals. It is recognisable from afar by two high-rise buildings – one the prestigious Hotel Arts – and Frank Gehry's enormous, shimmering copper fish. As you approach, passing a small park, the gleaming Hospital de Mar, and a *modernista* water tower, the promenade becomes increasingly lined with bars and restaurants. Here and in the **Port Olímpic**, just beyond, there are a number of good places to eat, and the proximity to beaches and boats is undeniably attractive, but the area has become over-commercialised and a bit tacky in parts.

Beyond the Olympic Port, development continues. There are more clean, sandy beaches and only a few of the old factories of the **Poble Nou** district have survived to be transformed into studios and apartments. Further still, **Diagonal Mar**, a project that has brought the Avinguda Diagonal down to the sea, has created a new residential district, demolishing old buildings and transforming wasteland. The Universal Forum of Cultures was held here in 2004 on an esplanade jutting out to sea. Its buildings, now used for congresses and other large-scale events, are a new landmark signalling the end of the city's waterfront.

Parc de la Ciutadella

Lodged between Port Olímpic and La Ribera is **Parc de la Ciutadella**, the city's largest park, which incorporates the city zoo, the **Parc Zoológic** (open daily 10am–5pm in winter, later in summer). This was the site, first, of the fortress built after the fall of Barcelona in 1714, and then of the 1888 World Exposition. Housed in a splendid *modernista* building designed for this event is the Zoological Museum. Nearby are the Geological Museum, the plant houses, the pretty Hivernacle and the Umbracle.

The popular park is always a relaxing refuge from the intensity of the city's streets. It's a lovely place, with an artificial lake where rowing boats can be hired, and shady benches beneath towering trees where parakeets, escaped from the Rambla cages, have taken control. The large baroque fountain, **La Cascada**, was designed by Josep Fontseré, whose assistant was a young architecture student named Antoni Gaudí. In the Plaça d'Armes is the Parlament de Catalunya. The autonomous government debates the issues of the day in a handsome building, once the arsenal of the 18th-century citadel.

From the park's inland exit on Pujades a broad promenade sweeps up to the

The fountain in Parc de la Ciutadella, partly designed by Gaudí

imposing **Arc de Triomf**, built as the entrance to the World Exposition. To the right, on Wellington, a new tram can be caught to Diagonal Mar. On the sea side of the park lies the grand Estació de França, the huge, ornate **Correus** (Post Office); and **La Llotja**, a centre of Barcelona's trading activities for more than 600 years. You can sometimes visit the building (tel: 93-319 24 12 for details), which has an attractive courtyard and a 14th-century Gothic hall.

Almost opposite is the splendid arcade of **Porxos Xifré**, a 19th-century complex that houses the **Set Portes Restaurant**, a Barcelona institution *(see page 140)*. If you head back from La Llotja towards the Rambla along the traffic-filled Passeig de Colom, you will pass the baroque splendour of **La Mare de Déu de la Mercè** church, which is best known because the sculpture of the Madonna on the dome can be seen for miles around and is something of a local landmark.

The sleek Museu d'Art Contemporani de Barcelona

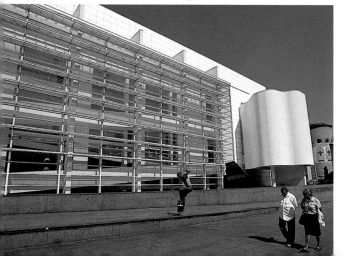

EL RAVAL

The district between La Rambla and the Ronda de Sant Antoni is **El Raval**, where numerous buildings have been demolished to create urban spaces and new housing in the latest trendy zone. From La Rambla, take Carrer del Carme, then turn right up Carrer dels Àngels to reach the most conspicuous symbol of this neighbourhood's transformation: Richard Meier's **Museu d'Art Contemporani de Barcelona** (MACBA; open Mon–Fri 11am–7.30pm, Sat 10am–8pm, Sun 10am–3pm), which is worth visiting for its architecture and the multicultural buzz in its square, where skateboarders, art lovers and locals all congregate. It is still working on putting together a serious contemporary collection, but it has some fine abstract works and good temporary exhibitions.

Next door is the ever-stimulating **Centre de Cultura Contemporània de Barcelona** (CCCB; open Tues–Sun 11am–8pm), a striking renovation of an old poor house, the Casa de Caritat. In this exciting space dance, music, film and other activities posit the urban experience as their theme.

Retrace your steps to Carrer del Carme and the Gothic complex of the **Antic Hospital de la Santa Creu** (Hospital of the Holy Cross), a hospital and refuge for pilgrims for a thousand years. Gaudí died here in 1926. The present structures were begun in 1401. Look for the frieze of 16th-century tiles on the life of St Paul in the entryway of the Institut d'Estudis Catalans. The courtyard is restful, with benches under orange trees ripe with fruit or fragrant with blossom. The Massana art school and the Library of Catalonia are both housed here.

Urban Regeneration

Carrer Hospital is a busy commercial street catering primarily to the Arab and Asian families living in the area. On and around it are some trendy little shops and restaurants, although the alleys do not look very inviting. On the far side of Hospital, the recently created Rambla del Raval leads down to Carrer Sant Pau. Old housing was demolished to make way for it, and new blocks, a film theatre and a 5-star hotel are being built as part of the urban regeneration process.

Off in a corner at the end of Carrer Sant Pau is the little church of **Sant Pau del Camp** (Mon–Sat 10am–1pm and 5–8pm, Sun 10am–4pm). The simplicity of its 12th-century Romanesque lines is an agreeable change from the extravagance of Barcelona's *modernisme* and the intricacies of Gothic architecture. It is believed to be the oldest church in the city. The lovely little cloister has curious, Arab-style arches.

MONTJUÏC

Montjuïc came into its own as the site of Barcelona's 1929 International Exhibition, and again for the 1992 Olympic Games. For many years its 210-m (689-ft) summit, panoramic view of the city and harbour, and outstanding complex of museums and sports facilities have made the hill a favourite spot. The Plaça d'Espanya is a good point to begin a visit to Montjuïc, as it has a metro and bus stop. A number of hangar-type halls, the premises of the Barcelona Trade Fairs organisation, line a central avenue leading upwards to the vast **Palau Nacional**, the fair's Spanish pavilion, and, in front of it, the **Font Màgica** (Magic Fountain), which performs a son et lumière show (May–Sept Thur–Sun

Elegant statue at the Pavelló Mies van der Rohe

The Magic Fountain and the imposing Palau Nacional

8–11.30pm; Oct, Dec–Apr Fri–Sat 7–9pm). Nearby is **Pavelló Mies van der Rohe** (open daily 10am–8pm), built for the 1929 Exposition, dismantled, then rebuilt in 1986. The glass, stone, and steel cube house is a wonder of cool Bauhaus forms.

Opposite is **Casaramona**, a magnificent *modernista* textile factory converted into the **Caixa Forum**, the Fundació la Caixa's wonderful cultural centre, with a full programme of exhibitions and concerts (Tues–Sun 10am–8pm).

National Treasures

External elevators make the ascent to the domed Palau Nacional easier. This is the **Museu Nacional d'Art de Catalunya** (MNAC; open Tues–Sat 10am–7pm, Sun 10am–2.30pm), housing one of the world's finest collections of Romanesque art. It has undergone extensive refurbishment over the past few years and holds 1,000 years of Catalan art, bringing together various collections under one roof, including part of the Thyssen-

Bornemisza collection, and the 19th- and 20th-century collection of the former Museu d'Art Modern de Catalunya.

Between the 9th and 13th centuries, over 2,000 Romanesque churches were built in Catalonia. Interiors were decorated with primitive sculptures of biblical episodes or rural life on the capitals of columns; painted altar panels; carved wooden crosses, and Madonnas of great purity. At the start of the 20th century many works were saved from deteriorating or abandoned churches and are now housed in the museum. There are masterpieces in every room. The Gothic wing is excellent, too. Many of the paintings are retablos, screens with arched frames that stood behind chapel altars. Among the treasures are Lluís Dalmau's Virgin of the Councillors (1445); Jaume Ferrer II's St Jerome; and a fine retable of St John the Baptist with saints Sebastian and Nicholas.

Miró sculpture outside the Fundació

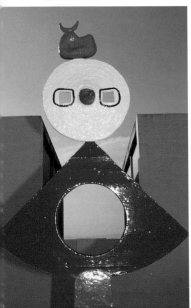

The 19th- and 20th-century collection includes Casas, Fortuny, Mir, Nonell and Rusiñol, though the most famous (Dalí, Miró, Picasso, Tàpies) are absent as they have museums of their own.

Museums and Miró

Up the hill is the **Museu Arqueològic** (open Tues–Sat 9.30am–7pm, Sun 10am–2pm). Among the exhibits, drawn mainly from prehistoric, Iberian, Greek and

Roman sites in Catalonia, are reconstructions of tombs and life-like dioramas. Around another curve, within walking distance uphill, is the **Museu Etnològic** (open Wed and Fri–Sun 10am–2pm, Tues and Thur 10am–7pm; summer Tues–Sat noon–8pm, Sun 11am–3pm). This well-presented collection usually has a special rotating programme highlighting the native arts of Latin America.

Further up lies the Jardins de Laribal (Montjuïc hill is covered with attractive gardens), and on the edge of it is the **Teatre Grec** amphitheatre, where the Festival Grec is held in June and July. Steps from here lead to the simple and elegant **Fundació Joan Miró** (open Tues, Wed, Fri and Sat 10am–7pm, Thur 10am– 9.30pm, Sun 10am–2.30pm). This excellent museum, which opened in 1975, was designed by the architect Josep Lluís Sert to house a large collection of paintings, drawings, tapestries and sculpture by the Catalan surrealist, who died in 1983 at the age of 90. The exhibits follow Miró's artistic development from 1914 onwards. Flooded with natural light, they are seen at their best. In the grounds outside are a number of his sculptures. The collection is witty and bright with the unique language symbols associated with the artist.

The Castell de Montjuïc, built in 1640, remained in use by the army, then as a prison until shortly before it was turned over to the city in 1960. The **Museu Militar** inside (open Tues–Sun 9.30am–8pm, until 5pm in winter) has an extensive

Cable cars

A funicular from Avinguda del Parallel metro station runs to Avinguda de Miramar (near the Fundació Joan Miró), and links up with the Telefèric, the newly renovated cable car which gives a ride with a view up to the Castell de Montjuïc. Another cable car, the Transbordador Aéri, runs from Montjuïc right across the port to Barceloneta (daily 10.45am– 6pm, weather permitting), stopping at the World Trade Centre.

The Torre de Calatrava

collection of antique weaponry and armour, lead soldiers from various epochs, and model castles.

The fort has sombre associations for the city: its cannons bombarded the population to put down rebellions in the 18th and 19th centuries, and it was the site of political executions, including that of Lluís Companys, president of the Generalitat of Catalonia during the Civil War, who was shot by a firing squad.

The **Anella Olímpica** (Olympic Ring) spreads across the northern side of Montjuïc and can be reached by an escalator from the Palau Nacional. The original 1929 Estadi Olímpic was enlarged for the 1992 Games. Near its entrance is the new Museu Olímpic i de l'Esport, a must for sports enthusiasts (open Wed–Mon 10am–8pm in summer, until 6pm in winter). Below the stadium is the Olympic Terrace; below that the colonnaded Plaça d'Europa.

Poble Espanyol

Off to the left is the high-tech **Palau d'Esports Sant Jordi**, designed by Japanese architect Arata Isozaki. It can seat 17,000 under a roof 45m (148ft) high. Towering over it all is the 188-m (616-ft) tall **Torre de Calatrava** communications tower.

Down the hill is the **Poble Espanyol** (Spanish Village; open Mon 9am–8pm, Tues–Thur 9am–2am, Fri–Sat 9am–4am, Sun 9am–midnight), a family attraction by day and a popular nightspot. Built for the 1929 Exposition, it's a composite of architecture representing Spain's varied regions, including replicas of houses, church towers, fountains, plazas and palaces arranged along a network of streets and squares. The entrance is through a gate of the walled city of Ávila. There is a flamenco show, restaurants, discos and demonstrations of regional crafts, including weaving, pottery and glass-blowing, which make it a good place to find well-made souvenirs.

THE DIAGONAL

The broad, tree-lined Avinguda Diagonal slices across Cerdà's grid from the coast to the hills linking up with the city ring roads. From the residential district Diagonal Mar a tram runs up to the area around the busy Plaça de les Glòries Catalanes roundabout. Nearby is Ricardo Bofill's neoclassical **Teatre Nacional de Catalunya** and Rafael Moneo's **L'Auditori**, a con-

The Teatre Nacional de Catalunya

Jean Nouvel's Torre Agbar
dominates the skyline

cert hall, which now includes the **Museu de la Música** (open Mon, Wed–Fri 11am–9pm, Sat–Sun 10am–7pm). The city's latest landmark, Jean Nouvel's gherkin-like **Torre Agbar**, is also here. The stretch between Passeig de Gràcia and Plaça de Francesc Macià is one of Barcelona's most elegant districts.

Pedralbes

Further up the Diagonal amid smart residential and office blocks is the **Palau Reial de Pedralbes**, a Güell-family estate converted into a royal residence in 1919. In a peaceful garden, it houses the **Museu de Ceràmica** and the **Museu de les Arts Decoratives** (open Tues–Sat 10am–6pm, Sun 10am–3pm). On the other side of the Diagonal is the Zona Universitària, and south of this, **Camp Nou Stadium**, home of Barcelona's revered football club, Barça, with a museum which includes a tour (open Mon–Sat 10am–6.30pm, Sun until 2.30pm).

Going up Avinguda de Pedralbes are Gaudí's **Pavellons Güell**, which contain a centre for the Ruta del Modernisme *(see page 50)*. At the top is the atmospheric **Monestir de Pedralbes** (open Tues–Sat, 10am–2pm, until 5pm in summer, Sun 10am–3pm). Founded in 1326 by Queen Elisenda de Montcada, whose tomb is in the superb Gothic church, it has a beautiful three-storey cloister.

The districts on the hillsides were once separate villages where residents of Barcelona spent summers and weekends.

They've been absorbed over the years, but each preserves its own character. Pedralbes is patrician – expensive, residential villas with gardens – while **Gràcia** has its own town square, the Plaça Rius i Taulet, and streets named Llibertat and Fraternitat and a Plaça Revolució, reflecting a political past. The Festa Major, held here for a week around 15 August, is one of the city's biggest. Sarrià retains the feel of a small Catalan town.

TIBIDABO

The first bright, clear morning or late afternoon of your visit, head for **Tibidabo**, the 542-m (1,778-ft) peak of the Collserola range, overlooking the city. The views are breathtaking. The church of **El Sagrat Cor de Jesus**, floodlit at night, built in the first half of the 20th century in neo-Romanesque

El Sagrat Cor de Jesus in Tibidabo

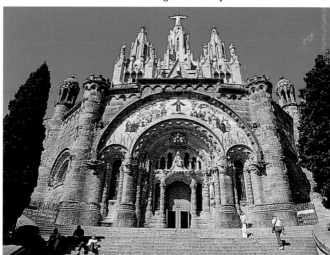

The spectacular view from the Torre de Collserola

and neo-Gothic style, and surmounted by a monumental figure of Christ, is one of the city's landmarks.

To reach the summit take the FGC train to Avda Tibidabo from the Plaça de Catalunya. From here a **Tramvia Blau**, an old-fashioned blue wooden tram, runs every day during the summer (weekends only in winter), taking you up to the funicular station, past stately mansions. En route, at Teodor Roviralta, you could stop at the **CosmoCaixa** (open Tues– Sun 10am–8pm), a splendid new science museum with lots to interest everyone. In five minutes the funicular (weekends only in winter) lifts you through pine woods to the top, where you have a spectacular panorama of the city, the coast and the Pyrenees.

Families flock to the famous, 1950s-style funfair, the **Parc d'Atraccions** (Easter–Dec Mon–Fri noon–10pm, Sat–Sun noon–midnight, but check with tourist office, as times vary) where every kind of ride and fairground attraction is on offer, including the TibiAir miniature plane. The **Museu d'Autò-mates**, displaying early slot machines and toys, is fun, too. The fair is just the best-known feature of the **Parc de Collserola**, a huge, green swathe that makes a great escape from the city. Families come here at weekends and summer evenings to enjoy the fresh air. There are jogging and cycling tracks, nature trails, picnic spots and *merenderos*, where you barbecue your own food.

Another high spot is the **Torre de Collserola** (open Wed–Sun 11am–2.30pm and 3.30–5pm) communications tower, sometimes known as the Torre Foster, after its architect, Sir Norman Foster who designed it for the 1992 Barcelona Olympics. A chic transparent lift whisks you to the top for fabulous panoramic views.

EXCURSIONS

There's a great deal to detain you in Bacelona, but just beyond the city there are several sites eminently worthy of day trips. These include the holy Catalan shrine of Montserrat, the relaxed and pretty town of Sitges for beaches and museums, and the cava wine country in the region of Penedès.

Montserrat

Montserrat, Catalonia's most important religious retreat and the shrine of Catalan nationhood, rises out of the rather featureless Llobregat plain 48km (30 miles) northwest of Barcelona. The view from its 1,235-m (4,050-ft) summit can encompass both the Pyrenees and Mallorca, and the monastery itself can be seen from afar, surrounded by jagged ridges which give it its name – the Serrated Mountain.

The first hermitages on the mountain may have been established by those trying to escape the Moorish invasion. One was enlarged as a Benedictine monastery in the 11th century and a century later it became the repository for **La Moreneta**, the Black Madonna, a small, wooden image of a brown-faced Virgin (darkened by candle smoke) holding the infant Jesus on her lap and a globe in her right hand. The figure is said to be a carving by St Luke, later hidden by St Peter. Ever since, pilgrims – from commoners to kings – have climbed the mountain to worship the Catalan patron saint. More than a million pilgrims and tourists visit the shrine each year.

The **monastery** (open daily 8.50am–7.30pm) was burned to the ground by Napoleon's soldiers in 1808, abandoned in 1835 when all convents were sequestered by the state, and rebuilt in 1874. During the Spanish Civil War, La Moreneta was secretly replaced by a copy; the original remained hidden during the dictatorship. Although Catalan culture was suppressed, monks here continued to say Masses in Catalan.

Montserrat's monastery, set high in the craggy mountains

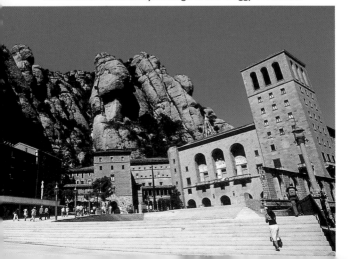

Vigils, Choirs and Cyclists

The site of the monastery is spectacular, tucked into folds of rock high above the plain. On the eve of the saint's day, 27 April, the monks hold an all-night vigil attended by huge crowds. La Moreneta looks down from a gold-and-glass case, above and to the right of the altar in the basilica, but the faithful can touch or kiss her right hand through an opening. At 11am, 1pm and 6.45pm (except in July), the Escolans, the oldest boys' choir in Europe, founded in the 13th century, fill the basilica with their pure voices. The monastery and its **museum** has a department of early art and a modern section, and contains many valuable works of art, include paintings by El Greco.

Montserrat is also the goal of cyclists (who make the trip from Barcelona) and mountain climbers who ascend the spires of rock above the building. From the monastery there are walks to other hermitages and a funicular to the **Santa Cova**, the cave sacred to the legend of the Madonna. Statues and plaques line the paths. Montserrat is extremely popular with tourists and pilgrims, so a number of bars, restaurants and shops have been set up around the Plaça de la Creu.

Getting There

Montserrat can be reached in an hour by FGC train from Barcelona's Plaça d'Espanya to either Montserrat Aeri where a cable car continues up the side of the mountain to the monastery, or the next stop, Monistrol de Montserrat, where the more comfortable Cremallera train goes up to the monastery, for the same price. There is a bus service from Sants bus station with Autocares Julià (tel: 93-490 40 00). If you are driving, leave Barcelona via the Diagonal and take the A2 highway in the direction of Lleida, exiting at Martorell.

The church of Sant Bartolomeu i Santa Tecla at Sitges

Sitges

It's easy to get to the Costa Daurada beaches from Barcelona.
The coast south of the city earned its name from its broad,
golden sands, in contrast to the rocky coves of the Costa
Brava to the north. **Sitges**, a favourite resort of Barceloneses, is the best place for a day trip. It's a short drive on the
C-32 motorway, or a 40-minute train ride from Sants or Passeig de Gràcia stations, if you get a fast train – some of them
stop frequently en route. There is also a scenic coastal drive
that is narrow and curvy and obviously takes longer.

Happily, the pretty little town has escaped the high-rises
and tawdry atmosphere of many coastal resorts, although it
does get somewhat overwhelmed by crowds in summer.
There are two beaches, separated by a promontory where
gleaming, whitewashed houses cluster around the church of
Sant Bartolomeu i Santa Tecla. The biggest and best beach
is **Platja d'Or** (Golden Beach), backed by a palm-lined prom-

enade and dozens of cafés and restaurants – some of them very good indeed. North of the promontory is Sant Sebastià beach, smaller and quieter and extremely pleasant.

Three Seaside Museums

Besides the beaches, Sitges is known for its appealing museums. The **Museu Cau Ferrat** (open summer Tues–Sun 10am–2pm and 5–9pm, winter Tues–Sat 9.30am–2pm and 3.30–6.30pm, Sun 10am–3pm) is in the house built by the painter Santiago Rusiñol (1861–1931), whose collection of works by El Greco, Casas, Picasso and others is on display, along with many of his own works.

Next to Cau Ferrat is the **Museu Maricel** (opening hours as above), a splendid house overlooking the sea – the name means 'sea and sky'. It displays a small collection of Gothic sculpture and paintings, some notable murals by Josep Maria Sert (1876–1945) and the town's art collection, with paintings by the Romantics, Lumanists and Modernists.

The nearby **Museu Romàntic** (opening hours as above), on Sant Gaudenci, displays the furniture and accoutrements of a wealthy 19th-century family, as well as a large collection of antique dolls, the Lola Anglada collection.

On the outskirts of Sitges are the villas of wealthy Barceloneses, while the pretty streets between the beach and station are geared for food and fun. Sitges has one of Spain's largest gay communities, and attracts gay travellers year-round, but particularly during the riotous February carnival.

Museu Marciel

The architecture's as good as the cava at Sant Sadurní

Gay and nudist beaches lie a little way beyond the other beaches of the town.

Locted inland from Sitges, on the road to Vilafranca, is **Sant Pere de Ribes**, which has a 10th-century castle and a delightful Romanesque church.

Sant Sadurní d'Anoia (Penedès)

Cava, Catalonia's sparkling wine, comes from the **Penedès**, a pretty region south of Barcelona (about 45 minutes on the train from Sants or Plaça de Catalunya stations; by road, take the AP2 and AP7 in the direction of Tarragona). These days the top-selling cavas are produced by Codorníu and Freixenet. The centre of cava production is the small town of **Sant Sadurní d'Anoia**, where several wineries offer guided tours and tastings.

The most interesting of these is **Can Codorníu** (open Mon–Fri 9am–5pm, Sat–Sun 9am–1pm; tel: 93-891 33 42 to check opening times in summer and to arrange a visit). This is Spain's largest producer of cava, and it has been in the business since 1872. The family-owned winery is located on a spectacular campus, with *modernista* buildings by Gaudí's contemporary, Puig i Cadafalch. Completed in 1898, it has been declared a National Artistic and Historic Monument. Visitors to the winery are taken on a theme-park-like ride through 26km (16 miles) of atmospheric underground cellars.

World-famous cava producer Freixenet has its headquarters next to the station and can be visited daily (tel: 93-891 70 96).

There are several good restaurants in and near town, which the staff at Codorniu will be happy to tell you about. Most of them specialise in seafood accompanied, of course, by cava. If you visit the area between January and March you must try another regional dish, *calçots* – baby leeks grilled and dipped in a peppery, garlicky sauce – and so popular they actually have a fiesta in their honour at this time, called the *calçotada*.

Vilafranca del Penedès

Some 15km (8 miles) to the south of Sant Sadurní, surrounded by vineyards, is **Vilafranca del Penedès**, the capital of the Alt-Penedès region and the place where the world-renowned Torres red wine is produced.

Inside the Museu del Vi

The **Museu del Vi** (open Sun 10am–2pm, Tues–Sat summer 10am–9pm, winter 10am–2pm, 4–7pm) is said to be one of the best wine museums in Europe, and is well worth a visit. It is housed in the Gothic **Palau Reial**, residence of the count-kings of Barcelona-Aragón.

The local festival (29 August to 2 September), when the wine flows freely and the human towers called *castells* make their appearance, is a good time to visit the town and a great way to round off your holiday.

WHAT TO DO

SHOPPING

Barcelona is firmly on the map of European shopping capitals. As a city of eminent style and taste, it is packed full of fashion boutiques, antique shops, state-of-the-art home interior stores and art galleries. Design is taken very seriously here. Shopping is also extremely pleasant, as the city has not been totally overtaken by homogenous chain stores, although there are some shiny new shopping malls. Catalonia still thrives on family-owned shops, and window shopping on the Rambla de Catalunya or Passeig de Gràcia is a delight. The best items include fashionable clothing, shoes and leather products; antiques; books (Barcelona is the publishing capital of Spain); high-tech design, home furnishings and objets d'art; and music.

Where to Look

Passeig de Gràcia, **Rambla de Catalunya** and **Diagonal** are great for fashion, jewellery and design. Art galleries and alternative fashion shops have sprung up on either side of **La Rambla**, in the Gothic Quarter, around **El Born** and in **El Raval**. Plaça de Catalunya is the jumping-off point for some of the best shopping streets. **Portal de l'Àngel** and **Carrer Portaferrisa** are always swarming with shoppers. The upper section of La Rambla has some leading fashion stores, though tacky souvenir shops are rife.

Festival fireworks over the Rambla del Mar footbridge

Shopping hours

With the exception of department stores, fashion stores and malls, most shops close 1.30–4.30pm, but all stay open until 8pm or later. Smaller shops may close on Saturday afternoon and most stores close on Sunday.

Department Stores and Malls

The major department store is **El Corte Inglés**, Spain's biggest. There is the huge, original branch on Plaça de Catalunya, one in Portal de l'Àngel, and one in the Diagonal (all open from 10am–10pm). Also in Plaça de Catalunya is a large complex called **El Triangle**, which includes a branch of Habitat, and a representative of the French chain, FNAC, which has the city's best selection of national and foreign music, books, DVDS and the very latest in computer wizardry. L'Illa, on the Diagonal, is one of Barcelona's best upscale shopping malls. VIPs in **Rambla de Catalunya** has a variety of shops and cafés. In **Port Vell**, the Maremàgnum mall is teeming with shops and stays open until 11pm. One of the largest and best equipped malls is **Diagonal Mar** by the sea near the Forum conference centre, easily reached by metro.

Antiques and Art Galleries

Some of the best spots for antiques are in the old town, along **Banys Nous**, **de la Palla**, and **Baixada Santa Eulàlia**, home to innumerable antiques dealers. In the Eixample, **Bulevar dels Antiquaris**, at Passeig de Gràcia 57, conceals a maze of dealers, and there are several individual shops on **Mallorca** and **Valencia**.

For art purchases, explore **Consell de Cent**, in the Eixample; the **Born**, a hot new gallery area; and the streets around the contemporary art museum, MACBA, in **El Raval**, where other galleries are springing up. There are several on **Petritxol**, near Plaça del Pi, and **Montcada**, clustered around the Picasso Museum. Ceramics, ranging from traditional tiles, plates and bowls with brightly coloured glazing, to more modern creations, can be found in the streets around the cathedral and along **Montcada**. A selection of good-quality ceramics and handicrafts is sold at Art Escudellers (Escudellers 23–25). BCN Original, next to the Tourist Information

Office at Plaça de Catalunya 17, has a nice selection of souvenirs and gifts. Many museum shops also sell high-quality art and design items.

Books

Spain's publishing industry is based in Barcelona, so it's easy to find a wide assortment of books, including many titles in English. Excellent books on Spanish culture, art and cookery and lots of discounted titles – many in English – are found at Happy Books (branches on Passeig de Gràcia, Pelai and at La Formiga d'Or in Portal de l'Àngel). Come In is an English bookshop on Provença, while Central in Elisabets is a haven for browsers, located in a former chapel. The Crisol chain (branch on Rambla Catalunya 81) is very well stocked, as is FNAC, on Plaça de Catalunya. There are excellent bookshops in the CCCB (Contemporary Culture Centre) and the MACBA in El Raval.

Hard to say which is nicer – the shop front or the pastries!

For all your musical needs

Design

For quintessential Catalan design, Vinçon (Passeig de Gràcia 96), Barcelona's top design emporium, is full of functional and well designed items – expensive lighting and funky furniture, cheaper watches, kitchen utensils and stationery. Pilma (Diagonal 403) has good stock and low-key good taste, but less innate style; and the Born area is good for trendy, original items notably Ici et La (Plaça Santa Maria 2) which specialises in local creatives.

Fashion

Cool fashion for men and women by Toni Miró can be found at his signature store (Antoni Miró) at Consell de Cent 349, and at Groc on Rambla de Catalunya 100. Galician designer Adolfo Domínguez sells classic fashion at Passeig de Gràcia 32 and 89 and Diagonal 570. Loewe in Casa Lleó Morera, Passeig de Gràcia 35, is Spain's premier leather goods store. Also good for leather (less expensive than Loewe) is Yanko, on Passeig de Gràcia 95. Also on Passeig de Gràcia, Gonzalo Comella sells labels including Miró, Armani and Ermenegildo Zegna.

Bulevard Rosa (Diagonal 474 and 609 and Passeig de Gràcia 55) has a number of excellent shops. For young and trendy clothes, you can't go wrong with Zara, a Spanish chain that has spread all over Europe. There are many branches, the biggest on Passeig de Gràcia at the junction with the Gran Via de les Corts Catalanes. Mango also has several outlets in the city. The area around Pelai and Portaferrissa is the hottest place for young fashion.

Food

Colmado Quílez (Rambla de Catalunya 63) is a classic Catalan emporium, with packaged goods, fine wines, cheeses and imported beer in a photogenic corner shop. For roasted nuts, dried fruits, coffee and spices, go to the 150-year-old Casa Gispert (Sombrerers 23) near Santa Maria del Mar. Escribà, at La Rambla 83, is a beautiful, century-old shop selling wonderful chocolates. For a religious experience and a history lesson with your shopping, visit Caelum (de la Palla 8), which stocks all kinds of products produced by monks (beers made by Trappist monks, honey, candles, cheese, etc). Downstairs is a cellar/tea room where ancient foundations of 14th-century baths were uncovered and are now on public view.

The ultimate food shopping experience in Barcelona, of course, is Mercat La Boqueria *(see page 26)* for fish, meat, fruit, vegetables, charcuterie and olives. It's open Monday to Saturday till 8pm and it's not to be missed.

Markets

Barcelona's biggest and best flea market is Els Encants, which pulsates with action every Monday, Wednesday, Friday and Saturday from 8am–7pm at Plaça de les Glóries Catalanes (Glóries Metro). Some of the stuff is good, some of it's rubbish, but it's all good fun. For stamps and coins and memorabilia, go to the Plaça Reial on Sunday morning, or to the Sant Antoni market for records and books. The Plaça Sant Josep Oriol has a weekend art fair and there is an Antiques Fair every Thursday in the cathedral square.

ENTERTAINMENT

Spaniards have earned a reputation as consummate party goers, and while Barcelona may not be quite as fanatical about late nights as Madrid, it is still a place that really comes to life when the sun goes down. It has virtually every kind of entertainment, from cool cabarets to live jazz, rock to flamenco and world music; as well as opera, symphony concerts, dynamic theatre and a thriving bar, club and disco scene. At night, some streets, such as the Rambla, become slow-moving rivers of people just walking and talking. The main churches and monuments are illuminated, and the city takes on a new and stimulating aspect.

Gran Teatre del Liceu

Music and Theatre

A concert at the **Palau de la Música** (Sant Francesc de Paula 2; tel: 902 44 28 82), the *modernista* masterpiece, is a wonderful experience, whatever the performance is. The varied programme includes chamber and symphony concerts, contemporary music and occasionally jazz.

Barcelona's famous opera house, **Gran Teatre del Liceu** (La Rambla 51–9, tel: 93-485 99 13 or 902 53 33 53, <www.liceubarcelona.com>), which was gutted by fire in 1994, reopened to general acclaim in 1999.

Tickets are hard to get, despite its increasing seating capacity, but worth a try. The **Auditori Municipal** (Plaça de les Arts), home of the Barcelona Symphony Orchestra, has a 2,500-seat auditorium and a smaller one for chamber concerts (for tickets, tel: 902 10 12 12 or 933 26 29 45 from abroad; <www.auditori.org>).

The **Caixa Forum**, Av. Marquès de Comillas 6 (tel: 902 22 30 40) is a sophisticated new cultural centre that hosts musical performances as well as exhibitions and other events.

For theatre, there is the **Teatre Nacional** (Plaça de les Arts, tel: 93-306 57 00), with a wide and varied programme; **Lliure** (Plaça Margarida Xirgu, tel: 93-228 97 47) for good contemporary productions; and **Mercat de les Flors** (Lleida 59, tel: 902 10 12 12), in a converted flower market, stages experimental theatre and contemporary dance. Naturally, most productions are in Spanish or Catalan but this obviously matters less with musicals.

Tickets for all cultural events can be booked at the information centre in Palau Virreina in La Rambla and, up to three hours before a performance, at the tourist office in Plaça Catalunya.

Flamenco and Jazz

Flamenco is not a Catalan tradition, but some *tablaos* – live flamenco performances – are staged for tourists. Tablao Flamenco Cordobés (Las Ramblas 35, tel: 93-317 57 11) is the most popular, while El Patio Andaluz (Aribau 242, tel: 93-209 33 78) also puts on *sevillanas*, traditional Andalusian music.

There are also shows twice nightly, except Monday, at El Tablao de Carmen in the Poble Espanyol on Montjuïc (Arcos 9, tel: 93-325 68 95). One of the most authentic shows is at Los Tarantos in Plaça Reial (tel: 93 3191789).

Live jazz can be found most nights at Harlem Jazz Club in the Gothic Quarter (Comtessa de Sobradiel 8), probably the city's best jazz club. Jamboree, in the Plaça Reial, is also good. Luz de Gas (Muntaner 246) presents jazz, rock and soul, and becomes a dance venue after midnight. Sala Apolo specialises in rock, pop and reggae.

Nightlife

For seasoned *juerguistas* (ravers) the Barcelona nightlife is hard to beat. From sundown to sunrise there's a venue for every taste and the streets buzz as if it were midday. For early evening don't miss Boadas (Tallers 1), an atmospheric 1930s cocktail bar famed for its mojitos, or a terrace bar in a square in the Gràcia neighbourhood, where a young, laid-back crowd gather.

The scene really hots up after midnight, much of it centred on the Old Town: Benidorm (Joaquín Costa 39) and Zentraus (Rambla del Raval 41) are both in the Raval, where a few remnants of the old Barri Xino mingle with hip new nightspots and restaurants like Rita Rouge (Plaça de la Gardunya) that turn into clubs at midnight. The Born area is still cool for classics like Gimlet (Rec 24) or Berimbau (Passeig del Born 17), while the Plaça Reial in the Gothic Quarter has every kind of bar from old favourite Glaciar, to restaurant-cum-lounge Club 13, or Sidecar which has live gigs. Uptown, some of the original 80s designer bars and clubs are still going strong, such as Otto Zutz (Lincoln 15) with its three dance floors and Ommsession, hip hotel Omm's club (Rosselló 265), the latest place to see and be seen. Irresistible in the summer are the beach bars or *chiringuitos* on every beach from Barceloneta to Diagonal Mar where you can dance in the sand till dawn.

Festivals

There are numerous music festivals: the **Festival de Música Antigua** in April and May (tel: 902 22 30 40), the **Festival de Guitarra de Barcelona** in May–June (tel: 902 10 12 12) and the **Grec Summer Festival** of dance, music and theatre. From the last week of June to the first week in August the cultural calendar is brimming with events ranging from avant-garde theatre to jazz concerts. Events are held all over the city, but the most impressive are at the **Grec Theatre**, an open air ampitheatre on Montjuïc (check programme and buy tickets at the Virreina, La Rambla 99).

If you're in the city during a festival you'll see the different neighbourhoods erupt into life. Food, fireworks, music and the huge papier-mâché effigies called *gegants* (giants) and their companions, the *cap grossos* (bigheads), are essential features. The *gegants* are about 4 metres (13 ft) high

Splendidly dressed *gegants* (giants)

and elaborately dressed as kings and queens, knights and ladies. *Cap grossos* are cartoon heads of well-known personalities, often accompanied by *dracs* (dragons) and *dimonis* (devils).

A constant of Catalan festivals are the *castellers*, acrobatic troupes of men, boys and girls who form human towers up to nine men high. This takes place most spectacularly at the **Festival of La Mercè**, the city's patron saint, on 24 September, in the Plaça de Sant Jaume. The **pre-Lent Carnaval** is another good excuse to dress up and hold processions and parties. Like most festivals it is accompanied by late-night bands and plenty of fireworks *(see page 94 for major events)*.

Enthusiastic Barça fans

SPORTS

Spectator Sports

The 1992 Olympics cemented Barcelona's reputation as a sports-mad city. Barceloneses are wild about Barça, their championship football (soccer) club, and are avid spectators of cycling, golf, and auto and motorcycle racing. But they're also active sports enthusiasts, eager to escape the city for cycling, sailing or skiing (only a couple of hours away in the Pyrenees). Recreational cycling on Montjuïc and Tibidabo is very popular, and of course swimming and sunbathing – whether at the city beaches or along the Costa Daurada and Costa Brava – is a prime activity.

The great spectator sport in Barcelona is football, and a match involving Barça, one of Europe's perennial champions, can bring the city to a standstill. The club's **Camp Nou** stadium, in the Les Corts area near the Diagonal, is the largest in Europe with a seating capacity of 120,000. Camp Nou has one of the most visited museums in Spain (open Mon–Sat 10am–6.30pm, Sun 10am–2.30pm).

Bullfighting

Bullfighting is not a Catalan passion, but Barcelona does have a bullring and *corridas de toros*, even if they don't grab the imagination of locals as they do in Madrid and the south of Spain. If you are interested, you can attend a bullfight at the Plaza de Toros Monumental (Gran Vía Marina), on Sunday afternoon at 5pm during the summer.

Participant Sports

Visitors can jog in Montjuïc or Tibidabo, rent skates or bikes, or play golf at one of the fine courses near the city. Alternatively, visit Tibidabo's **Can Caralleu sports centre** (tel: 93-204 69 05 for opening hours for non-members), which has tennis, pelota, volleyball and two swimming pools.

Cycling is popular and tourist offices can provide a map showing recommended routes and bike lanes and advice about taking bikes on public transport. Or contact **Amics de la Bici**, Demóstenes, 19, tel/fax: 93-339 40 60. On Tibidabo, the **Carretera de las Aiguas**, a path that winds along the mountain with spectacular views of the city below, is a great place to walk, jog or cycle. **Barcelona by Bicycle** offers easygoing tours around La Ribera, the Gothic Quarter and the waterfront – one even includes dinner (tel: 93-268 21 05 for more information). They also hire bikes. Bikes can be rented from **Icària Sports**, Av. Icària 180, tel: 93-221 17

78; and from **Filicletos**, Passeig de Picasso 40, tel: 93-319 78 11, where there is easy access to the Parc de la Ciutadella and the waterfront (tandems and child seats available).

At the **Reial Club de Golf El Prat**, El Prat de Llobregat, tel: 93-379 02 78 near the airport, 27 holes provide three different circuits. Clubs and carts may be rented, and there's a pool for non-participants. Other courses located nearby include that of the **Club de Golf Sant Cugat**, Sant Cugat del Vallès, tel: 93-674 39 08/93-674 39 58, just west of the city, which hires clubs and trolleys and has a pool; and the **Terramar course** at Sitges, tel: 93-894 05 80. For additional information, visit <www.catgolf.com>.

For sailing information, you can contact the **Reial Club Marítim**, tel: 93-221 48 59. For watersports and equipment hire in general, try **Base Nautica de la Mar Bella**, Platja de Bogatell, Av. Litoral, tel: 93-221 04 32.

Skiing in the Pyrenees is popular; most resorts are within two hours of Barcelona, some are accessible by train, and there are cheap weekend excursions available. Information can be obtained from the **Asociació Catalana d'Estacions d'Esquí**, tel: 93-416 09 09, or <www.lamolina.com>.

FOR CHILDREN

Barcelona is an excellent city for children. For one thing, taking young children to restaurants is a regular occurence, so they are completely accepted, even late into the evening. The clean beaches will keep most children and parents happy, in between sightseeing excursions; and the Port Vell waterfront has **L'Aquàrium**, one of the largest aquariums in Europe with some fascinating marine life on display (Moll d'Espanya, tel: 93-221 74 74). There is also a **3-D Imax** movie theatre in the port (tel: 902 33 22 11). The **Zoo** (Ciutadella Park, tel: 93-221 25 06), is not the world's greatest, but it's in a pleasant setting. The park itself, with boats for hire, is fun and shady.

The **Poble Espanyol** (Montjuïc), a re-creation of a Spanish village, is popular with families, both locals and visitors, and manages to interest teenagers as well as children.

Tibidabo amusement park (Parc d'Atraccions tel: 93-211 79 42) is good, old-fashioned entertainment, and kids love to arrive there on the Tramvia Blau *(see page 72)*. As for museums, the science museum **CosmoCaixa** below the park is full of hands-on, child-friendly exibits, including an area dedicated to 3–6-year-olds *(see page 72)*. The **Museu de la Xocolata** (Chocolate Museum), Antic Convent de Sant Agustí, La Ribera, has tempting chocolate sculptures; and the **Museu de Cera** (Wax Museum) off la Rambla at Passatge de la Banca 7, tel: 93-317 26 49, with its lifelike models, is usually a hit, as well.

Fun at the fair in Tibidabo

Calendar of Events

5–6 January Reis Mags (Three Kings' Day), gift giving and procession.

February (second week) Feast of Santa Eulàlia. Winter Festa Major – low key version of La Mercè (see 24 Sept).

Feb–March Carnival, preceding Lent, is a wild celebration. Sitges carnival is the best in the region.

Setmana Santa/Easter Palm Sunday procession along Rambla de Catalunya. Processions and services on Holy Thursday/Good Friday.

23 April Feast of Sant Jordi (St George), book and flower stalls are set up in La Rambla and Passeig de Gràcia.

27 April Feast of Virgin of Montserrat, liturgical rituals, choir singing and *sardana* dancing.

11 May Sant Ponç; herb fair in Carrer de l'Hospital.

mid-June Corpus Christi, carpets of flowers and processions in Sitges. In Barcelona 'dancing eggs' are balanced on the spray of the cathedral fountain and fountains in other courtyards in the Barri Gòtic.

23–24 June Sant Joan (St John), a major event in Catalonia, with fireworks, feasting and flowing cava.

late June–early August Grec Summer Festival of theatre, dance, classical, pop and rock music.

15–21 August Festa Major de Gràcia, street parties, parades, fireworks and flags in Gràcia neighbourhood.

11 September Diada, Catalan national day, with demonstrations and flag waving.

24 September La Mercè. Barcelona's week-long festival, in honour of its patron, Mare del Déu de la Mercè (Our Lady of Mercy). Fireworks, dancing and music in the streets. The Ball de Gegants is a parade of huge papier-mâché figures; Correfoc is a rowdy nocturnal parade of devils and fire-spitting dragons, not to be missed. *Castells* in Plaça St Jaume.

6–22 December Santa Llùcia Fair selling Nativity figurines, art, crafts and Christmas trees in front of the cathedral.

26 December Sant Esteve (St Stephen's Day). Families meet for an even larger meal than that eaten on Christmas Day.

EATING OUT

Catalans adore eating, and especially love dining out, the epitome of social activity. They enjoy one of the finest, most imaginative cuisines in Spain, and Barcelona is the best place to sample its rich variety. The cooking is an attractive mix of haute cuisine and the traditional rustic cooking that has fed Catalans for centuries.

Barcelona's restaurants begin with a major advantage: superb ingredients, as anyone who's entered a great covered market in the city can attest. Catalan cooking is based on *cuina del mercat* – market cuisine. Fresh fish and shellfish lead the menus (even though they're often flown in from the north coast and Galicia). Fruits and vegetables are at their freshest. Mountain-cured hams and spicy sausages, spit-roasted meats and fowl with aromatic herbs are specialities. Expect *all i oli* (garlic and olive oil mayonnaise), produce from the countryside, and wild mushrooms – *bolets* – an object of obsession for people from all over Catalonia.

Barcelona's cosmopolitan population enjoys food of every Spanish region; Basque cookery is especially appreciated and Basque tapas bars have sprouted like the much-loved wild mushrooms. International cuisine used to mean French, but the number of restaurants from all over the world has exploded. Most top restaurants are in the Old Quarter and the Eixample, though the most lively area is

Los Caracoles has been feeding Barcelonans for decades

Enjoying tapas

along the waterfront, in the new port and in El Born. The most exclusive restaurants tend to be in the Barrios Altos residential neighbourhoods north of the Eixample. Eating out in Barcelona is a treat and can be one of the highlights of your trip. Restaurants are not cheap, but they compare favourably with those in many European and North American capitals. Sometimes menus are offered only in Catalan, so always ask if there is one in English or Spanish.

Meal Times and Menus

Barceloneses, like all Spaniards, eat late. Lunch usually isn't eaten until 2.30 or 3pm. Dinner is served from about 9pm until 11.30pm, although at weekends people sometimes don't sit down to dinner until midnight. You can usually get a meal at almost any time of the day, but if you enter a restaurant soon after the doors have swung open, you are likely to find yourself dining alone, or with other foreign visitors. You could always adopt the Spanish system, which is to pace yourself for the late hours by eating tapas.

Barceloneses often eat a three-course meal at both lunch and dinner, including dessert and coffee. However, it's not uncommon to share a first course, or to order *un sólo plato* – just a main course. Many restaurants offer a lunchtime *menú del día* or *menú de la casa*, a daily set menu that is a really good bargain. For a fixed price you'll get three courses: a starter, often soup or salad, a main dish, and dessert (ice-cream, a piece of fruit or the ubiquitous *flan*, a kind of caramel custard), plus wine, beer or bottled water, and bread. Typically, the cost is about half what you'd expect to pay if you ordered from the regular menu. Many Spaniards also order the *menú*, so there's no need to think you're getting the 'tourist special'.

You can also eat cheaply in cafeterías, where you will usually be offered a *plat combinat* (*plato combinado* in Spanish), usually meat or fish with chips and salad, served on the same plate. Not the best way to eat, but fast and inexpensive.

Reservations are recommended at Barcelona's more popular restaurants. Prices generally include service, but it's customary to leave a 5–10 percent tip.

Restaurants feature a grading system, from one to five forks, marked on the door; signs are supposed to announce the category as well, though they are not always prominently displayed. The system indicates price, and grades the facilities and service, not the quality of the food.

Your choices are not limited to restaurants and cafeterias. Most bars (also called *tabernas*, *bodegas* and *cervecerías*) serve food, often of a surprisingly high standard. Here you can have a selection of tapas, sandwiches (*bocadillos* in Span-

Tapas

Tapas – the snacks for which Spanish bars and cafés are world-famous – come in dozens of delicious varieties, from appetisers such as olives and salted almonds, to vegetable salads, fried squid, garlicky shrimps, lobster mayonnaise, meatballs, spiced potatoes, wedges of omelette, sliced sausage and cheese. The list is virtually endless, and can be surprisingly creative, especially at the now extremely popular Basque tapas joints.

A dish larger than a tapa is called a *porción*. A large serving, meant to be shared, is a *ración*, and half of this, a *media ración*. Best of all, tapas are usually available throughout the day, and are a great way to try new tastes.

ish, *bocats* or *entrepans* in Catalan) or limited *plats combinats* at almost any time of the day.

Breakfast is a trivial affair in most of Spain, Barcelona included, except at hotels that offer mega-buffets as money-makers or enticements. (Check to see if breakfast is included in the room price at your hotel; if not, it's probably better to try the nearest café or cafetería.) Local people usually have a *café con leche* accompanied by bread, toast, a pastry or croissant. The occasional bar and cafetería may serve an 'English breakfast' of bacon and eggs.

Local Specialities

The foundation of rustic Catalan cuisine is *pa amb tomàquet* – slices of rustic bread rubbed with garlic and halves of beautiful fresh tomatoes, doused with olive oil, and sprinkled with coarse salt. Another typical Catalan dish is *espinacs a la cata-*

Eating in La Boqueria market

lana, spinach prepared with pine nuts, raisins and garlic. Others include *escudella* (a thick tasty Catalan soup); *suquet de peix* (fish and shellfish soup); *botifarra* (Catalan sausage, often with white beans); *fuet* (long, salami-type sausage); and *fideus* (long, thin noodles served with pork, sausage and red pepper). A popular local fish served in a variety of ways is *rape* (angler fish), especially tasty prepared *a l'all cremat* (with roasted garlic). Other good bets are *llobina al forn* (baked sea bass) and *llenguado a la planxa* (grilled sole). You might be fooled by the Catalan word for a Spanish *tortilla* (omelette), which is *truita*, but translates as both omelette and trout. *Bacallà*, the lowly salt cod, is now served in the most distinguished restaurants in various guises. A *sarsuela* is a stew of fish cooked in its own juices; a *graellada de peix* is a mixed grill of fish.

Other specialities are *llebre estofada amb xocolata* (stewed hare in a bitter-sweet chocolate sauce). Barcelona's all-purpose sausage is the hearty *botifarra*, often served (in spring) with *faves a la catalana* (young broad beans stewed with bacon, onion and garlic in an earthenware casserole). *Xató* (pronounced *sha-toe*) is the endive and olive salad of Sitges, fortified with tuna or cod, and has an especially good sauce made of red pepper, anchovies, garlic and ground almonds. The word for salad of any kind is *amanida*.

Although it originates in rice-growing Valencia, the classic seafood paella is high on many visitors' lists of dishes to sample in Barcelona. Try the restaurants in Barceloneta for a paella of fresh mussels, clams, shrimp and several kinds of fish. It will take about 20 minutes to prepare.

When it comes to dessert, *flan* is ubiquitous, but there's a home-made version, the more liquid *crema catalana* (egg custard with caramelised sugar on top). *Mel i mato* is a treat made with honey and creamy cheese. The greatest sweet things are the delightful delicacies sold in pastry shops.

Winebar in the Barri Gòtic

Drinks

Wine is a constant at the Catalan table. In addition to an assortment of fine wines from across Spain, Barcelona presents an opportunity to try some excellent regional wines. Penedès, the grape-growing region just outside Barcelona, produces some excellent wines, including cava, Spain's sparkling wine. Cava goes well with seafood and most tapas. Among Penedès reds, try Torres Gran Coronas, Raimat and Jean León. Wines from the Priorat area are superb, robust, expensive reds that rival the best in Spain. Don't be surprised to be offered red wine chilled in hot weather.

Sangría is a favourite, made of wine and fruit fortified with brandy, but it's drunk more by visitors than locals. Spanish beers, available in bottles and on draft, are generally light and refreshing. A glass of draught beer is a *caña*.

You'll find every kind of sherry *(jerez)* here. The pale, dry *fino* is sometimes drunk not only as an apéritif but also with soup and fish courses. Rich dark *oloroso* goes well after dinner. Spanish brandy varies from excellent to rough: you usually get what you pay for. Other spirits are made under licence in Spain, and are usually pretty cheap. Imported Scotch whisky is fashionable, but expensive.

Coffee is served black *(solo)*, with a spot of milk *(cortado/tallat)*, or half and half with hot milk *(con leche)*. There is the usual array of international soft drinks available, and sometimes freshly squeezed orange juice. *Horchata de chufa*, made with ground tiger nuts, is a popular summer drink. *Horchaterías* are bars specialising in *horchata* and ice cream.

To Help you Order

Could we have a table?	**¿Nos puede dar una mesa, por favor?**
Do you have a set menu?	**¿Tiene un menú del día?**
I'd like a/an/some…	**Quisiera…**
The bill, please	**La cuenta, por favor**

Deciphering the Menu

agua	water	**gambas**	prawns
al ajillo	in garlic	**helado**	ice cream
a la plancha	grilled	**jamón serrano**	cured ham
al punto	medium		
arroz	rice	**judías**	beans
asado	roasted	**langosta**	lobster
atún	tuna	**leche**	milk
azúcar	sugar	**lomo**	pork loin
bacalao	dried cod	**mariscos**	shellfish
bocadillo	sandwich	**mejillones**	mussels
boquerones	anchovies	**morcilla**	black pudding
buen hecho	well done	**pan**	bread
buey/res	beef	**pescado**	fish
calamares	squid	**picante**	spicy
cangrejo	crab	**poco hecho**	rare
caracoles	snails	**pollo**	chicken
cerdo	pork	**postre**	dessert
cerveza	beer	**pulpitos**	baby octopus
champiñones	mushrooms	**queso**	cheese
chorizo	spicy sausage	**salsa**	sauce
cocido	stew	**sepia**	cuttlefish
cordero	lamb	**ternera**	veal
ensalada	salad	**tortilla**	omelette
entremeses	hors-d'oeuvre	**trucha**	trout
flan	caramel custard	**verduras**	vegetables
		vino	wine

HANDY TRAVEL TIPS

An A–Z Summary of Practical Information

A

ACCOMMODATION *(Hoteles; alojamiento;* see also the list of
RECOMMENDED HOTELS starting on page 128)

New hotels open regularly in Barcelona, but rooms can still be hard
to find if a congress is on. Advance reservations are strongly recommended. Spanish hotels are rated by a star system, with five-star
deluxe the top grade. The classifications often seem arbitrary, with
some two- and three-star places just as good as others rated higher.
About two-thirds of the city's hotels fall into the three- and four-star
categories. Breakfast is rarely included in the rate. For economy bud-
gets, there are several hundred star-rated guest houses *(hostales, pen-
siones)* and youth hostels *(albergues de juventud)*. Accommodation
can be booked through the tourist office in Plaça de Catalunya.

I'd like a double/single room.	**Quisiera una habitación doble/sencilla.**
with/without bath/shower double bed	**con/sin baño/ducha cama matrimonial**
What's the rate per night?	**¿Cuál es el precio por noche?**
Is breakfast included?	**¿Está incluído el desayuno?**
Where's an inexpensive hotel?	**¿Dónde hay un hotel económico?**

AIRPORTS *(Aeropuertos)*

Barcelona's international airport, **El Prat de Llobregat** (tel: 902 404
704) is 12 km (7 miles) south of the city. The distribution of flights
in the three terminals may vary, so confirm from which your flight
will depart. There are tourist information and hotel reservation booths
in Terminals A and B (open daily 9am–9pm; tel: 93-478 47 04).

You can get into Barcelona by train, bus or taxi. The national train
service, RENFE (tel: 902 240 202), runs trains from the airport to

Estació de França every half hour, stopping at Estació de Sants and Passeig de Gràcia, taking about 30 minutes. The fare is about €1.25. The Aerobús departs every 12 minutes from all three terminals for Plaça de Catalunya, Mon–Sat 6am–11pm, Sun 6.30am–10.45pm, stopping at several points en route. The fare is about €4 single, €7 return; tel: 93-412 00 00. Taxis, lined up outside the terminals, charge about 25 euros to the centre of the city. Make sure you have agreed a fare before you start.

RyanAir (<www.ryanair.com>) flies to **Girona** (90km/56 miles from Barcelona) and **Reus** (80km/50 miles from Barcelona) from several UK cities. Both have shuttle-bus connections to Barcelona (check timetables on the following websites – Girona: <www. sagales.com>; Reus: <www.hispanoigualadina.net>). Tickets are available at the airports and the journeys take 60–90 minutes depending on traffic.

B

BICYCLE RENTAL (Alquiler de bicicletas)

Bicycle lanes are well marked out in the city's main streets. Cycles can be rented at several outlets, such as Icària Sports, Avenida Icària 180, tel: 93-221 17 78; and from Filicletos, Passeig de Picasso 40, tel: 93-319 78 11, where there is easy access to the Parc de la Ciutadella and the waterfront (tandems and child seats available). Barcelona by Bicycle, tel: 93-268 21 05, offers tours around La Ribera, the Gothic Quarter, and the waterfront – one even includes dinner. They also hire bikes. Contact Amics de la Bici, Demóstenes, 19, tel/fax: 93-339 40 60 for more information.

BUDGETING FOR YOUR TRIP

Barcelona is, on the whole, cheaper than other major European cities such as London, Paris or Rome, but it has become much more than expensive than it used to be.

Transport to Barcelona. For Europeans, Barcelona is a short, direct flight away. As well as regularly scheduled flights there is a good choice of discounts and charter flights, especially those booked on the Internet, e.g. EasyJet at <www.easyjet.com>. For those travelling from outside Europe, the flight will be a considerably greater proportion of your budget, but you may be able to find packages and specials.

Accommodation. Hotels in Barcelona, along with Madrid, are the most expensive in Spain, but many at the three- and four-star level are comparatively good value. Most do not include breakfast or the 7 percent IVA (value added tax). See approximate prices in the Recommended Hotels section, starting on page 128.

Meals. Restaurant prices are not cheap, but even top-rated establishments are reasonable compared to many European capitals. The *menú del día*, a fixed-price midday meal, is an excellent bargain and in new establishments give young chefs a chance to shine. Spanish wines are usually reasonably priced, even in fine restaurants.

Local transport. Public transport within the city – buses and the metro – is inexpensive *(see page 121)* and taxis are reasonably priced.

Incidentals. Your major expenses will be excursions, entertainment and daytime sporting activities. There is a moderate charge for nearly all museums and galleries, with some inter-museum deals available (see <www.articketbcn.org>). Nightclub and disco cover prices are high, as are drink prices once inside.

C

CAR HIRE *(Coches de alquiler)*

Unless you plan to travel a good deal throughout Catalonia, there is no need to rent a car (the excursions on *pages 73–9* are all easily accessible by public transport). Barcelona has considerable parking problems and general congestion, and a car is more trouble than it's worth.

If you do wish to rent a car, however, major international companies – Avis, Hertz, Budget, National – and Spanish companies, have offices in the airport and in the city centre. A value-added tax (IVA) of 15 percent is added to the total charge, but will have been included if you have pre-paid before arrival (normally the way to obtain the lowest rates). Fully comprehensive insurance is required and should be included in the price; confirm that this is the case. Most companies require you to pay by credit card, or use your card as a deposit/guarantee. You must be over 21 and have had a licence for at least 6 months. A national driver's licence will suffice for EU nationals; others need an international licence.

I'd like to rent a car for tomorrow for one day/a week	**Quisiera alquilar un coche para mañana por un día/una semana**
Please include full insurance.	**Haga el favor de incluir el seguro a todo riesgo.**
Fill it up, please.	**Lleno, por favor.**
May I return it to the airport?	**¿Puedo dejarlo al aeropuerto?**

CLIMATE

Barcelona's mild Mediterranean climate assures sunshine most of the year and makes freezing temperatures rare even in the depths of winter (December to February). Spring and autumn are the most agreeable seasons for visiting. Midsummer can be hot and humid; at times a thick smog hangs over the city. Average temperatures are given below.

	J	F	M	A	M	J	J	A	S	O	N	D
°F	49	51	54	59	64	72	75	75	71	63	56	51
°C	9	10	12	14	18	22	24	24	22	18	13	11

CLOTHING *(Ropa)*

Barceloneses are very stylish and fashion-conscious. Smart-casual clothing is what visitors generally need. Men are expected to wear a jacket in better restaurants. Jeans and sports shirts are fine in informal bars and restaurants, but you won't see many local people eating out in shorts and trainers, except in beach-side cafés. From November to April you'll need a warm jacket or sweater and raincoat. The rest of the year, light summer clothing is in order.

CRIME AND SAFETY (see also EMERGENCIES on page 111)

You should exercise caution and be on your guard against pickpockets and bag snatchers (be wary of people offering 'assistance'), especially on or near La Rambla, the old city (particularly El Raval) and other major tourist areas, such as La Sagrada Família and crowded spots such as markets. Avoid deserted alleyways, especially at night.

Don't leave luggage unattended; don't carry more money than you'll need for daily expenses; use the hotel safe for larger sums and valuables; photocopy personal documents and leave the originals in your hotel; wear cameras strapped crosswise on your body; don't leave video cameras, car stereos and valuables in view inside a car, even when locked.

The blue-clad, mobile anti-crime squads are out in force on the Ramblas and principal thoroughfares. Should you be the victim of a crime, make a *denuncia* (report) at the nearest police station *(comisaría* – vital if you are going to make an insurance claim). The main one in the Old Town is at Nou de la Rambla 76–78, or call the Mossos d'Esquadra on 088 or 112.

I want to report a theft.	**Quiero denunciar un robo.**
My handbag/wallet/ passport has been stolen.	**Me han robado el bolso/ la cartera/el pasaporte.**
Help! Thief!	**¡Socorro! ¡Ladrón!**

CUSTOMS AND ENTRY REQUIREMENTS *(Aduana)*

For members of EU countries the process is easy: you won't even get your passport stamped (although you still need to carry it). Visas are needed by non-EU nationals unless their country has a reciprocal agreement with Spain. Full information on passport and visa regulations is available from the Spanish Embassy in your country.

As Spain is part of the EU, free exchange of non-duty-free items for personal use is permitted between Spain and other EU countries. However, duty-free items are still subject to restrictions. There are no limits on the amount of money that you may import. Visitors may bring up to €6,000 into or out of the country without a declaration. If you intend to bring in and take out again larger sums, declare this on arrival and departure.

D

DRIVING

In the event of a problem, drivers have to produce a passport, a valid driving licence, registration papers and Green Card international insurance.

Road Conditions. Roads within Barcelona are very congested and the ring roads around the city can be confusing. Roads and highways outside Barcelona, along the coast and through the interior of Catalonia and to the Pyrenees, are excellent, though you'll have to pay a toll *(peaje/peatje)* on most motorways *(autopistas)*. When crossing the La Jonquera border with France (160 km/100 miles) from Barcelona, take the A7 motorway. For road information, tel: 900 123 505.

Rules and Regulations. Your car should display a nationality sticker. Front and rear seatbelts, a spare set of bulbs, visibility vests and two warning triangles are compulsory. Most fines for traffic offences are payable on the spot. Driving rules are the same throughout Europe: drive on the right, overtake on the left, give right of way to vehicles coming from the right (unless your road is marked as having priority). Speed limits are 120 km/h (75 mph) on motorways, 100 km/h (62 mph) on dual carriageways, 90 km/h (56mph) on main roads, 50 km/h (30 mph), or as marked, in urban areas.

The roads are patrolled by the Traffic Civil Guard (Guardia Civil de Tráfico) on motorcycles. Courteous and helpful, they are also tough on lawbreakers. Don't drink and drive. The permitted blood-alcohol level is low and penalties stiff.

Fuel. Service stations are plentiful. Petrol *(gasolina)* comes in 95 (Euro super lead-free), and 98 (lead-free super plus) grades, at most but not all petrol stations. Diesel fuel is widely available.

Road signs. Most signs are the standard pictographs used throughout Europe. However, you may encounter the following written signs in Spanish, often amended in Catalan:

¡Alto!	Stop!
Aparcamiento	Parking
Autopista	Motorway
Ceda el paso	Give way (yield)
Cruce peligroso	Dangerous crossroads
Curva peligrosa	Dangerous bend
Despacio	Slow
Peligro	Danger
Prohibido adelantar	No overtaking (passing)
Prohibido aparcar	No parking

Parking. Finding a place to park can be extremely difficult in Barcelona. Look for 'blue zones' (denoted by a blue 'P'), which are metered areas; or underground parking garages (also marked with a big blue-and-white 'P'). Green zones are reserved for residents with permits.

Breakdowns and Assistance. Emergencies, tel: **112**. On motorways there are SOS boxes. Garages are efficient, but repairs may take time.

Spare parts are readily available for Spanish-built cars and other popular models. For other models, they may have to be imported.

Registration papers	**Permiso de circulación**
Is this the right road for…?	**Es ésta la carretera hacia…?**
Full tank, please.	**Lléne el depósito, por favor.**
normal/super	**normal/super**
Please check the oil/ tyres/battery.	**Por favor, controle el aceite/ los neumáticos/la batería.**
Can I park here?	**¿Se puede aparcar aquí?**
My car has broken down.	**Mi coche se ha estropeado.**
There's been an accident.	**Ha habido un accidente.**
(International) Driving Licence	**Carnet de conducir (internacional)**
Car-registration papers	**Permiso de circulación**
Green card	**Tarjeta verde**

E

ELECTRICITY *(Corriente eléctrica)*

The standard is 220 volts, but some hotels have a voltage of 110–120 in bathrooms as a safety precaution. Check before plugging in any of your appliances.

Power sockets (outlets) take round, two-pin plugs, so you will probably need an international adapter plug. Visitors from North America will also need a transformer, unless they have dual-voltage travel appliances.

What's the voltage?	**¿Cuál es el voltaje?**
an adapter/a battery	**un transformador/una pila/una batería**

EMBASSIES AND CONSULATES *(Embajadas y consulados)*

Almost all Western European countries have consulates *(consulados)* in Barcelona. All the embassies are in Madrid.

Australia: Gran Vía Carles III, 98, 9°, tel: 93-330 94 96.

Canada: Calle Elisenda de Pinós 10, tel: 93-204 27 00.

Ireland: Gran Vía Carles III, 94, tel: 93-491 50 21.

UK: Avinguda Diagonal 477, 13°, tel: 93-366 62 00.

US: Passeig de la Reina Elisenda 23, tel: 93-280 22 27.

EMERGENCIES (see also EMBASSIES AND CONSULATES, HEALTH AND MEDICAL CARE, POLICE, and CRIME AND SAFETY)

Emergency numbers:

General emergencies: 112

Mossos d'Esquadra (Autonomous Catalan Police): 088

Municipal (city) police: 092

Fire: 080

Ambulance: 061

Careful!	**¡Cuidado!**	Police!	**¡Policia!**
Fire!	**¡Fuego!**	Stop!	**¡Para!/¡Deténagase!**
Help!	**¡Socorro!**	Thief!	**¡Ladrón!**

G

GAY AND LESBIAN TRAVELLERS *(Homosexual; gay; lesbiana)*

Barcelona has an active gay community and scores of clubs and nightlife options. Conservative Catholic beliefs still predominate, though, in many sectors, so gay visitors may wish to be discreet. The gay and lesbian hotline is 900 601 601. The free magazine *Nois* has information and listings of clubs, restaurants and other entertainment options. Casal Lambda, Verdaguer i Callis 10, tel: 93-319 55 50, email: <infor@lambaweb.org>, is a gay cultural centre (open from 5pm).

GETTING THERE

By Air (see also AIRPORTS)

Barcelona's airport is linked by regularly scheduled daily non-stop flights from across Europe. Some flights from the US and Canada are direct; others go through Madrid (or in some cases, Lisbon). From Australia and New Zealand, regular one-stop flights go directly to Barcelona or Madrid. Flying times: London, about 2 hours; New York, approximately 8 hours.

Iberia, the Spanish national airline, covers most countries in shared arrangements with their own carriers. Contact Iberia in the UK at: Iberia House, 10 Hammersmith Broadway, London W6 7AL, tel: 08456 012 854. They are a member of Opodo, the internet online booking service that gives the cheapest deals among a number of national carriers (<www.opodo.co.uk>). Some very good charter airline deals can be found, especially if booked via the Internet. There are frequent scheduled flights between Barcelona and Madrid and other Spanish cities on Iberia (tel: 902 40 05 00), Spain's privately owned airline, Air Europa (tel: 902 401 501) and budget airline Vueling (<www.vueling.com>).

International Airport is El Prat de Llobregat (tel: 902 404 704), 12 km (7 miles) south of the city centre.

By Sea

Visitors usually arrive in Barcelona by sea only if coming from the Balearic Islands. Buquebus (tel: 971 40 09 69 fax: 971 29 10 09; <www.buquebus.com>) is the fastest Mallorca ferry (3 hours). Departures from Barcelona are Mon–Thur at 8am; Fri and Sat at 8am and 4pm. Return trips from Palma, Mallorca leave Fri and Sun at 8pm and midnight, other days at 7.30pm. Transmediterránea (Moll Sant Bertran 3, tel: 93-295 91 00; <www.trasmediterranea.es>) also operates ferries to the Balearic islands; most of the year they take about 8 hours but in summer, there's an express ferry that takes about 4 hours.

By Rail

Passengers generally have to change trains at the Spanish frontier, as the Spanish tracks are of a wider gauge than the French. Exceptions are the luxury high-speed TALGO and the Trenhotel, which have adjustable axles. These trains are efficient and modern and are a pleasant way to get to Barcelona (<www.raileurope.co.uk>).

The TALGO and Trenhotel arrive at Estació de França (near Parc de la Ciutadella; Metro: Arc de Triomf). The rest go to Estació Sants (Metro: Sants). RENFE is the Spanish national rail network; tel: 902 240 202, <www.renfe.es> for national services, tel: 902 24 34 02 for international trains. Local trains in Catalonia are serviced by the Catalan government, Ferrocarrils Generalitat de Catalunya (FGC; tel: 93-205 15 15).

RENFE honours Inter-Rail, Rail-Europ and Eurail cards (the latter sold only outside Europe), and offers substantial discounts to young people under 26 and senior citizens (over 65). It is well worthwhile finding out about current discount tickets from a travel agency, local railway station, or, in Barcelona, from the information desk in Sants station or by phoning RENFE on the number given above.

By Car

The highways outside of Barcelona are generally excellent, and cars travel very fast. The AP7 motorway leads to Barcelona from France and northern Catalonia, the AP2 leads to Barcelona from Madrid, Zaragoza and Bilbao. From Valencia or the Costa del Sol, take the E-15 north.

GUIDES AND TOURS (Guías; visitas guiadas)

English-speaking, licensed guides and interpreters may be arranged through the Barcelona Guide Bureau (tel: 93-268 24 22; email: <bgb@bcn.servicom.es>) or City Guides (tel: 93-412 06 74). Hotels and travel agencies will also advise on guides and interpreters.

Tours by bus: Barcelona Bus Turístic offers a tour of 44 city sights with three different routes; get on and off as you please. Buses depart from Plaça de Catalunya at 9am daily; all stops have full timetables. Complete journey time is about 3 hours. The bus runs year-round except for 25 December to 1 January. Tickets may be purchased on-board or in advance at Turisme de Barcelona, Plaça de Catalunya, tel: 93-285 38 34.

On foot: Barcelona Walking Tours has English-speaking, guided tours of the Gothic quarter every Saturday and Sunday at 10am. Walks (lasting 90 minutes) begin at Turisme de Barcelona, Plaça de Catalunya, tel: 93-285 38 34. At 10.30am on Saturdays and Sundays there is also a Picasso tour. Walks should be booked in advance at a tourist office.

By bicycle: Barcelona by Bicycle (Espartería 3, tel: 93-268 21 05) leads easy-going bike tours around the Old City and the waterfront (one tour includes dinner). The Montjuïc 'mcard' which gives reduced prices for museum entry, also includes bike hire.

HEALTH AND MEDICAL CARE

Standards of hygiene are high, and medical care in Barcelona is generally excellent; most doctors speak sufficient English. The water is safe to drink, but bottled water is always safest (and tastes better); it is inexpensive and available everywhere. *Agua con gas* is carbonated, *sin gas* is still water.

Visitors from EU countries with corresponding health insurance facilities are entitled to medical and hospital treatment under the Spanish social security system – you need a European Health Insurance Card, obtainable from post offices or online. However, it does not cover everything and it is advisable to take out private medical insurance, which should be part of a travel insurance package.

In an emergency, go to the 'Urgencias' department of a main hospital: Hospital Sant Pau, Carrer Sant Antoni Maria Claret 167, tel:

93-436 47 11 (behind the Sagrada Família); Hospital Clinic, Carrer de Casanova 143, tel: 93-227 54 00; Hospital Cruz Roja, Carrer Dos de Maig 301, tel: 93-433 15 51.

For an ambulance, make your way to an *ambulatorio* (medical centre) or tel: **061**.

Pharmacies *(farmacias)* operate as a first line of defence, as pharmacists can prescribe drugs and are usually adept at making on-the-spot diagnoses. Pharmacies open during normal business hours but there is always one in each district that remains open all night and on holidays. The location and phone number of this *farmacia de guardia* is posted on the door of all the others, and carried in daily newspapers. Tel: **010** for this information.

Where's the nearest (all-night) pharmacy?	**¿Donde está la farmacia (de guardia) más cercana?**
I need a doctor/dentist.	**Necesito un médico/dentista.**

HOLIDAYS *(Fiestas)*

1 January: Año Nuevo	New Year's Day
6 January: Epifanía/Los Reyes	Epiphany
1 May: Fiesta de Trabajo	Labour Day
24 June: San Juan	St John's Day
15 August: Asunción	Assumption
11 September: La Diada	Catalan National Day
24 September: La Mercè (Mercedes)	Barcelona's patron saint
1 November: Todos los Santos	All Saints' Day
6 December: Día de la Constitución	Constitution Day
8 December: Inmaculada Concepción	Immaculate Conception
25–26 December: Navidad	Christmas

Movable dates:

Feb/March: Mardi Gras	Shrove Tuesday (Carnival)
late March/April: Viernes Santo	Good Friday

late March/April: Lunes de Pascua	Easter Monday
mid-June: Corpus Christi	Corpus Christi

I

INTERNET

There are numerous sites in Barcelona where internet access is cheap and easy. Try: easyInternet Café at La Rambla 31 and Ronda Universitat 35, <www.easyinternetcafe.com>, both branches open 24 hours a day; Net-Movil, La Rambla 130, tel: 93-342 42 04, email: <netmovil@yahoo.com>, open daily 10am–midnight; email from Spain, La Rambla 42, tel: 93-481 75 75, email: <jmg@emailfrom spain.es>, open Mon–Sat 10am–8pm; and BCNET Internet Gallery Café, Barra de Ferro 3 (near the Picasso Museum), tel: 93-268 15 07, email: <bcnetcafe@bcnetcafe.com>.

L

LANGUAGE (Idioma; lenguaje)

Both Catalan (catalá) and Castilian Spanish (castellano) are official languages in Catalonia; everyone in Barcelona who speaks Catalan can speak Castilian Spanish, but because many residents come from other parts of the country they do not all speak Catalan. Catalan has experienced a huge renaissance, which has much to do with the people's cultural identity, and many of them will not speak Castilian Spanish unless it is absolutely necessary. Street signs are in Catalan, but museum labels and menus are usually in both languages.

Learning some phrases in Catalan will be appreciated, but Spanish (Castilian) will certainly get you by, which is why most of the language tips in this section are given in Spanish.

The Berlitz Spanish Phrase Book and Dictionary covers most situations you are likely to encounter during your stay in Barcelona, and includes a menu-reader supplement.

English	*Catalan*	Castilian
Good morning	*Bon dia*	**Buenos días**
Good afternoon	*Bona tarda*	**Buenas tardes**
Goodnight	*Bona nit*	**Buenas noches**
Goodbye	*Adéu*	**Adiós**
Hello	*Hola*	**Hola**
See you later	*Fins despr'es*	**Hasta luego**
Please	*Si us plau*	**Por favor**
Thank you	*Gràcies*	**Gracias**
You're welcome	*De res*	**De nada**
Welcome	*Benvinguts*	**Bienvenido**
Do you speak English?	*¿Parla anglés?*	**¿Habla inglés?**
I don't understand.	*No ho entenç*	**No entiendo**
How much is it?	*¿Quant es?*	**¿Cuánto vale?**
Open/closed	*obert/tancat*	**abierto/cerrado**

MAPS *(Planos)*

Since 1985, all street names in Barcelona and most Catalan towns have been posted in Catalan. Several towns have reverted to their Catalan names, too. Lérida is Lleida, San Carlos is Sant Carles, etc. Many maps published earlier than 1985 still have names in Spanish and even quite different names. Many Barcelona streets are one-way and/or do not permit turns to the left or right. A good, detailed street map will be of immense assistance if you are driving. The *Guía Urbana de Barcelona* handbook is the most comprehensive and useful.

I'd like a street plan/ a road map of this region	**Quisiera un plano de la ciudad/ un mapa de carreteras de esta región**

MEDIA *(Periódico = newspaper; revista = magazine)*

Most European newspapers and the Paris-based *International Herald Tribune* are sold on the day of publication at newsstands in the Ramblas and Passeig de Gràcia and in FNAC in Plaça de Catalunya. Principal European and American magazines are also widely available. *Metropolitan*, Barcelona's first monthly magazine in English is free and has useful listings. For Spanish speakers the *Guía del Ocio (Leisure Guide)* lists bars, restaurants, and cinema, theatre and concert performances.

Most hotels and bars have television, usually tuned to sports (international or local), in Castilian and Catalan. Most hotels offer multiple channels (German, French, Sky, BBC, CNN). Reception of the BBC World Service radio is usually good.

MONEY *(Dinero)*

Currency *(moneda)*. The monetary unit of Spain is the euro (symbolised €). Notes are issued in denominations of 5, 10, 20, 50, 100, 200 and 500 euros. Coins in circulation are 1, 2, 5, 10, 20 and 50 cents and 1 and 2 euros.

Currency exchange *(cambio)*. Banks and *cajas/caixes* (savings banks) are the best place to exchange currency, offering the best rates with no commission. Many travel agencies and *casas de cambio* (displaying a *cambio* sign) will also exchange foreign currency, and stay open outside banking hours *(see opposite)*. Be wary of those advertising 'no commission' – their rates are much lower, so you are in effect paying a hefty commission. Banks and exchange offices pay slightly more for travellers' cheques than for cash. Always take your passport when you go to change money.

Credit cards *(tarjetas de crédito)*. Most major international cards are widely recognised, though smaller businesses tend to prefer cash. Photo identification is usually requested when paying with a card. They are also useful for obtaining cash advances from banks. A credit card will usually give you the highest exchange rate, translated at the time of billing rather than the moment of transaction.

ATMs. Cash machines are ubiquitous in Spain and you'll find them all over Barcelona. In several languages, they will dispense money against your cash or credit card in just the same way that they do at home, using the same PIN number.

Travellers' cheques *(cheques de viajero)*. Throughout Barcelona, hotels, shops, restaurants and travel agencies all cash travellers' cheques, and so do banks, where tourists are practically guaranteed to get a better rate – you will always need your passport. Try to cash small amounts at a time, and keep the individual numbers of your cheques separately so they can be replaced quickly if they are lost or stolen.

Where's the nearest bank/ currency exchange office?	**¿Dónde está el banco/ la casa de cambio más cercana?**
I want to change some pounds/dollars	**Quiero cambiar libras/dólares**
Do you accept travellers' cheques?	**¿Acceptan cheques de viajero?**
Can I pay with a credit card?	**¿Se puede pagar con tarjeta?**
How much is that?	**¿Cuánto es/Cuánto vale?**

OPENING HOURS

Shops. The bigger stores and shopping malls open 10am–9.30pm, but most shops close in the early afternoon (for lunch). Usual hours are Mon–Sat 9am–1.30pm and 4–8pm, although these do vary.

Post offices. Usually open Mon–Fri 9am–2pm, Sat 9am–1pm *(also see Post Offices, page 120)*.

Banks. Generally open Mon–Fri 8.30am–2pm, and Sat 9am–1pm during the winter.

Government offices and most businesses. Open Mon–Fri 9am–2pm and 4–8pm. In summer, many businesses work *horas intensivas*, which means they open from 8am–3pm, to avoid the hottest part of the day.

Museums. Most open Tues–Sat 9am–1pm and 4–8pm in winter (many remain open through lunchtime in summer) and Sun 10am–2.30pm. Most close on Mondays, but there are exceptions.

P

POLICE *(Policía)*

The municipal and autonomous Catalan police are efficient and courteous – and generally very responsive to issues involving foreign tourists. In Barcelona, dial **092** for municipal (city) police and **088** for the autonomous Catalan police. The main police station in the Old Town is at Nou de la Rambla 76–78.

Where's the nearest police station?	¿Dónde está la comisaría más cercana?

POST OFFICES *(Correos)*

Post Offices – identified by yellow-and-white signs with a crown and the words 'Correos y Telégrafos' – are for both mail and telegrams; but you can't usually telephone from them. The postal system has greatly improved in recent years and is now pretty reliable. Opening hours are usually Mon–Fri 9am–2pm and Sat 9am–1pm. The Central Post Office, in Plaça Antoni López, at the port end of Via Laietana in the port area, tel: 93-216 04 53, is open Mon–Fri 9am–9pm and Sat 9am–1pm.

Stamps *(sellos)* can be purchased at the post office or more easily at *estancos/ estancs* (tobacconists) – look for the brown-and-yellow sign that reads 'Tabacs'. Rates are divided into four areas of the world, just like telephone calls: the EU, rest of Europe, the US and Canada, and the rest of the world. Allow about one week for delivery to North America, and 4–5 days to the UK. To speed things up, send a letter *urgente* (express) or *certificado* (registered).

Where is the Post Office?	**¿Dónde está el Correo?**
A stamp for this letter/	**Por favor, un sello para esta**
postcard, please.	**carta/tarjeta postal**
I'd like to send this letter.	**Me gustaría enviar esta carta.**
airmail	**vía aérea**
express (special delivery)	**urgente**
registered	**certificado**
How long will it take to	**¿Cuánto tarda en llegar?**
arrive?	

PUBLIC TRANSPORT *(Transporte público)*

Barcelona has a reliable and comprehensive public transport system; getting around town is easy, rapid and inexpensive. Tel: **010** for information on all public transport (Mon–Sat 8am–10pm).

By Metro. The metro is excellent, modern and clean, and by far the fastest and easiest way to navigate the city. Barcelona has begun to implement tri-lingual directions and audio (in Spanish, Catalan and English). Stations are marked by a red diamond symbol. Single-ticket fares and 10-trip tickets *(see page 122)* are available, the latter working out at nearly half-price the equivalent in single tickets. The metro runs Mon–Thur 5am–11pm, Fri and Sat 5am–2am; holidays 6am–11pm and Sun 6am–midnight. Good pocket-sized maps are available at metro stations.

By Bus *(autobús).* About 70 bus routes criss-cross Barcelona. Routes and hours are clearly marked at the stops but if it is your first time in the city, the bus may not be the best option. You'll have trouble recognising where you are, and most bus drivers speak no

English. With the metro, at least you can clearly identify your stop. But buses are a good way of getting to see more of the city. They run daily 6am–11pm; there are infrequent night buses from 10.30pm–5am. You can buy a single ticket from the driver, or purchase a multiple card *(tarjeta multi-viaje T-10)*, which is punched once you are inside the bus. This is valid for bus, metro and urban FGC lines and allows transfer from one means of transport to the other with no extra charge, within a time limit. Buy the T10 at stations, banks or *estancs (see above)*.

The official Tourist Bus, which passes numerous interesting sights in the city is excellent; you can jump on and off at any stop *(see page 114)*. An air-conditioned bus, rather unfortunately called the 'Tomb Bus', runs during business hours from the Plaça de Catalunya to the uptown Plaça Pius XII, covering all the smart shopping areas.

By Train. Suburban FGC (Ferrocarrils Generalitat de Catalunya) trains are useful for reaching Barcelona's upper neighbourhoods Gràcia, Sarrià, Pedralbes and Tibidabo and nearby towns such as Terrassa and Sabadell. These run from Plaça de Catalunya, but from a different station to the metro. Be careful not to confuse them. The FGC trains also run from Plaça Espanya to Montserrat, Colònia Güell and other destinations.

By Taxi. Black-and-yellow taxis are everywhere and not too expensive. During the day, they aren't your best option, as traffic is very heavy in the city. At night, especially if you've dined in the old

When's the next bus/ train to…?	**¡Cuándo sale el próximo autobús/tren para…?**
bus station	**estación de autobuses**
A ticket to…	**Un billete para…**
single (one-way)	**ida**
return (round-trip)	**ida y vuelta**
How much is the fare to…?	**¡Cuánto es la tarifa a …?**

quarter, taxis are the best way to return to your hotel or continue on with the night (have the restaurant call if you don't feel comfortable waiting for one on the street). Hail a cab in the street or pick one up where they're lined up (usually outside hotels). A green light and/or a *libre* (vacant) sign shows when the cab is empty.

Reputable taxi companies include Radio Móvil (tel: 93-358 11 11), Radiotaxi Verd (tel: 93-266 39 39) and Taxigroc (tel: 93-490 22 22). Check the fare before you get in; rates are fixed and are displayed in several languages on the window. Also ensure that the meter has been re-set when you begin your journey. Refuse a cab if the driver claims the meter is not working.

R

RELIGION *(Religión; servicios religiosos)*

Roman Catholicism is the religion of Catalonia (and all Spain) and Mass is said regularly in the churches of Barcelona. There are churches of most major faiths; the tourist information office at Plaça de Catalunya has information on religious services, including those in foreign languages. Major ones are: Anglican: St George's Church, Sant Joan de la Salle 41, tel: 93-417 88 67 (Sunday, 11am); Judaism: The Synagogue, Avenir 24, tel: 93-200 61 48; Islam: Centro Islàmico, Avinguda Meridiana 326, tel: 93-351 49 01.

T

TELEPHONES *(Teléfonos)*

Spain's country code is **34**. Barcelona's local area code, **93**, must be dialled before all phone numbers, even for local calls.

You can make direct-dial local, national and international calls from public phone booths *(cabinas)* in the street. Most operate with coins and cards; international phone credit cards can also be used. Instructions for use are given in several languages in the booths. For most calls at payphones, it's easier to use a phone card *(tarjeta telefónica)*, which can be purchased at any post office or *estanc* (look for the sign 'Tabacos' or 'Tabacs').

To make an international call, dial **00** for an international line + the country code + phone number, omitting any initial zero. The country code for the UK is 44, for the US and Canada it is 1, and for Australia, 61. Calls are cheaper after 10pm on weekdays, after 2pm on Saturday, and all day Sunday. For general telephone information, dial **1003**. For international calls, dial **1005,** for national calls, **1009**.

You can also make calls at public telephone offices called *locutorios*. These are much quieter than making a call on the street. A clerk will place the call for you and you pay for it afterwards.

Local, national, and international calls can also be made from hotels, but almost always with an exorbitant surcharge. Make them with an international calling card, if you must make them from your hotel room. (Before departure, be sure to get the international access code in Spain for your long-distance telephone carrier at home.)

You can send a fax from the main post office or from most hotels, although the charges can be high in the latter. Most *locutorios* and stationers also offer a fax service.

TIME ZONES

Spanish time is the same as that in most of Western Europe – Greenwich Mean Time plus one hour. Daylight Saving Time is in effect from the last Sunday in March to the last Sunday in October; clocks go forward one hour in spring and back one hour in autumn, so Spain is generally one hour ahead of London, the same as Paris, and six hours ahead of New York.

TIPPING *(Propina; servicio)*

Since a service charge is normally included on hotel and restaurant bills, tipping is not obligatory but it's usual to leave small change (about 5 percent of the bill) on a bar counter, and 5–10 percent on restaurant bills. If you tip taxi drivers, 5 percent is enough unless they are especially helpful. Additional guidelines:

Hotel porter, per bag	60 cents
Lavatory attendant	25 cents
Tour guide	10 percent
Hairdresser	10 percent
Maid	60 cents–€1

TOILETS

There are many expressions for toilets in Spanish: *aseos, lavabos, servicios* and *WC*. The first two are the most common. Toilet doors are distinguished in Catalan by an 'H' for *Homes* (men) or 'D' for *Dones* (women) or by a variety of pictographs.

In addition to the well-marked public toilets in main squares and stations, a number of neat coin-operated toilets in portable cabins marked 'WC' are installed around the city. Just about every bar and restaurant has a toilet available for public use. It is considered polite to buy a drink if you drop in to use the conveniences.

Where are the toilets?   **¿Dónde están los servicios?**

TOURIST INFORMATION *(Oficinas de información turística)*

Tourist Offices Abroad
Canada: 2 Bloor St. West, Suite 3402, Toronto, Ontario M4W 3E2, tel: 416-961 31 31
UK: Spanish Tourist Office, 79 New Cavendish Street, London W1W 6XB, tel: 020-7486 8077; brochure line: tel: 09063 640 630; this office is open to the public by appointment only.
Catalan Tourist Office, 17 Fleet Street (3rd Floor), London EC4Y 1AA, tel: 020-7583 8855.

US: Water Tower Place, Suite 915 East, 845 North Michigan Avenue, Chicago, IL 60611, tel: 312-642 1992;

8383 Wilshire Boulevard, Suite 960, 90211 Beverly Hills, CA 90211, tel: 323-658 7195;

666 5th Avenue, 35th floor, New York, NY 10103, tel: 212-265 88 22;

1395 Brickell Avenue, Miami, FL 33131, tel: 305-358 19 92.

Barcelona Tourist Offices

For general information, tel: **010**, once in Barcelona, or from abroad tel: 93-285 38 34. The main tourist office is Turisme de Barcelona, Plaça de Catalunya 17, below ground; hotel information tel: 93-304 32 32; open daily 9am–9pm.

The Tourism Information Office in the Ajuntament (Town Hall), Plaça Sant Jaume, is open Mon–Sat 8am–8pm, Sun and public holidays 8am–2pm.

Informació Turística de Catalunya, Palau Robert, Passeig de Gràcia 107, tel: 93-238 40 00; <www.gencat.es/probert> provides information about Catalonia; open Mon–Fri 10am–7pm, Sat 10am–2pm.

There are also offices at Sants Station, open Mon–Sat 8am–10pm, the Airport, tel: 93-478 47 04, open Mon–Sat 9.30am–8pm, Sun 9.30am–3pm and a stand on La Rambla.

Where is the tourist office?   **¿Dónde está la oficina de turismo?**

WEBSITES

The following websites will provide you with plenty of useful information about Barcelona before you start your trip:

• Barcelona Ajuntament (City Hall): <www.bcn.es> the excellent official site which includes everything from hotels to 'what's on'.

- Barcelona Tourist Information: <www.barcelonaturisme.com>
- Catalonia on the web: <www.gencat.es>
- Spain on the web: <www.spaintour.com>
- National Tourist Office: <www.tourspain.es>
- Transport information: <www.tmb.net> or <www.renfe.es>.

Most of the major museums have their own websites; if you log on to one of the sites above you will be directed to them; or simply insert the name of the museum in which you are interested, and search the web. Most of the larger hotels now have websites and these have been given in the Hotels and Restaurants section starting on *page 128*.

WEIGHTS AND MEASURES

Like the rest of Europe, Spain uses the metric system. As a rough guide, there are 5 litres to 1 imperial gallon and about 4 litres to 1 US gallon; 1 kilogram equals 2.2lbs and 10 km is 16 miles. Clothes in most stores now have labels showing UK and US as well as continental European sizes; and shoe sizes are generally given in US and UK measurements as well.

YOUTH HOSTELS

The following youth hostels get very busy in the summer months, so it is advisable to book in advance if you can.

Albergue Juvenil Palau, Carrer Palau 6, tel: 93-412 50 80.

Gothic Point, Carrer Vigatans, tel: 93-268 78 08, fax: 93-310 77 55.

Hostal de Joves: Passeig de Pujades 29, tel/fax 93-300 31 04 (near Parc de la Ciutadella).

Kabul, Plaza Reial 17, tel: 93-031 851 90, fax: 93-419 301 40 34.

Mare de Déu de Montserrat, Mare de Déu de Coll 41–52, tel: 93-210 51 51, fax: 93-210 07 98.

Pere Tarrès, Numància 149, tel: 93-410 23 09, fax: 93-419 62 68.

Recommended Hotels

Many new hotels, mostly of the four- and five-star category, have been built in Barcelona both before and since the 1992 Olympic Games. Fears that there would be a glut of rooms have not been realised, as the city has continued to increase in popularity.

Hotels of greatest interest to most visitors are those in the Eixample, the commercial and *modernista* grid north of Plaça de Catalunya, or in the Ciutat Vella, which includes La Rambla and the Barri Gòtic. Many visitors choose to stay on or near La Rambla, though they have to tolerate late-night noise and crowds. Most mid-level to luxury hotels are either along La Rambla or in the Eixample.

Accommodation can get booked up early, even out of season, so always make bookings well in advance.

Weekend rates and special deals are available at many hotels. Most hotel rates do not include breakfast or iva, the 7 percent value-added tax. The following guide indicates prices for a double room in high season (prices should be used as an approximate guide only):

€€€€	over 240 euros
€€€	115–240 euros
€€	65–115 euros
€	below 65 euros

EIXAMPLE

Alexandra Hotel €€€ *Carrer de Mallorca 251, tel: 93-467 71 66, fax: 93-488 02 58, <www.hotel-alexandra.com>*. A business-like hotel between Rambla de Catalunya and Passeig de Gràcia – an excellent location. Rooms are not large, but they are comfortable and nicely furnished. Wheelchair access. 103 rooms and 6 suites.

Astoria Hotel €€€ *Carrer de París 203, tel: 93-209 83 11, fax: 93-202 30 08, <www.derbyhotels.es>*. Part of the prestigious Derby chain. A sophisticated and quiet hotel, just a few paces from prime shopping territory on the Diagonal. Built in the 1950s, the Astoria has been thoroughly refurbished and is now extremely elegant –

certainly one of the best three-star hotels in Spain. Some rooms have small sitting rooms or garden terraces. Wheelchair access. 117 rooms.

Avenida Palace Hotel €€€€ *Gran Vía de les Corts Catalanes 605, tel: 93-301 96 00, fax: 93-318 12 34, <www.avenidapalace. com>*. The place to stay if Barcelona's high-tech design craze seems too functional and cold. A luxurious, ornate hotel in the heart of the Eixample, on a busy thoroughfare. Rooms are spacious and elegant. Popular with upscale tour groups. Wheelchair access. 160 rooms.

Balmes Hotel €€€ *Carrer de Mallorca 216, tel: 93-451 19 14, fax: 93-451 00 49, <www.derbyhotels.es>*. Another Derby Hotel, the Balmes promises 'the advantages of the countryside in the heart of the city', and has an attractive leafy garden and a pool. Close to all the *modernista* masterpieces. It has a collection of African art and contemporary paintings. 100 rooms, all with parquet flooring.

Hotel Barcelona €€€ *Carrer de Casp 1–13, tel: 93-302 58 58, fax: 93-301 86 74*. A stone's throw from Passeig de Gràcia and Plaça de Catalunya, this is a functional choice for small groups and business travellers. Wheelchair access. 72 rooms.

Claris Hotel €€€€ *Carrer de Pau Claris 150, tel: 93-487 62 62, fax: 93-215 79 70, <www.derbyhotels.es>*. Another in the Derby chain, this is one of Barcelona's most elegant and expensive hotels, in the heart of the Eixample. Very high-tech design behind the facade of the Vedruna Palace and guests-only museum of Egyptian art. Rooms, many of which are split-level and even two-storey, exude cool chic, combining antiques and Catalan design. Small rooftop pool. Wheelchair access. 120 rooms.

Condes de Barcelona Hotel €€€€ *Passeig de Gràcia 73–5, tel: 93 467 47 80, fax: 93 467 47 85, <www.condesdebarcelona.com>*. With an ultra-chic address, just a block from Gaudí's La Pedrera, this popular hotel occupies two impressive former palaces on opposite corners. Rooms are modern, large and elegant, decorated in bright colours. A favourite of architects, designers, as well as European and Japanese tourists. Wheelchair access. 183 rooms.

Ducs de Bergara €€€€ *Carrer de Bergara 11, tel: 93-301 51 51, fax: 93-317 34 42, <www.hoteles-catalonia.com>.* A luxury, four-star hotel just off Plaça de Catalunya, in a handsome 19th-century townhouse expanded to seven floors. The hotel has a relaxed but elegant feel, and service is top-notch, although the rooms are quite small. Swimming pool in an inner courtyard. Wheelchair access. 150 rooms.

Gran Hotel Havana Silken €€€€ *Gran Vía de les Corts Catalanes 647, tel: 93-412 11 15, fax: 93-412 26 11, <www.hotelessilken.com>.* A hip and high-tech hotel in an 1872 mansion situated on Gran Via. Deluxe accommodation at a not unreasonable price. Barcelona's signature design elements are in every detail. Wheelchair access. 145 rooms.

Granvia €€–€€€ *Gran Via de les Corts Catalanes 642, tel: 93-318 19 00, fax: 93-318 99 97, <www.nnhotels.es>.* A small, intimate hotel with Old World style, occupying a 19th-century palace in a choice location, the Granvia has been operating since the 1930s. Smallish but clean rooms, furnished with antiques. Good value. Parking. Wheelchair access. 54 rooms.

Majestic €€€€ *Passeig de Gràcia 68, tel: 93-488 17 17, fax: 93-488 18 80, <www.hotelmajestic.es>.* A large, long-time favourite, the Majestic has recently been refurbished from the ground up. Two excellent restaurants – one is the exclusive Drolma. Wheelchair access. 331 rooms.

Omm €€€€ *Rosselló 265, tel: 93-445 40 00, fax: 93-445 40 04, <www.hotelomm.es>.* Just off Passeig de Gràcia, this award-winning designer hotel is for the chic and beautiful, or those who aspire to be. The rooms are stylish and well lit, the rooftop pool is stunning with views of Gaudí's La Pedrera, and the in-house club is the latest place to be on Barcelona's night scene. 59 rooms.

Hotel Palace €€€€ *Gran Vía de les Corts Catalanes 668, tel: 93-510 11 30, fax: 93-318 01 48, <www.ritzbcn.com>*. A 1919 belle époque hotel, this former Ritz is a classic place to stay. Ultra-luxurious and white-glove grand, on a splendid tree-lined avenue. Formal guest rooms, some with marble fireplaces. A couple even have Roman-style baths with rich mosaics. Wheelchair access. 127 rooms.

Regente €€€ *Rambla de Catalunya 76, tel: 93-487 59 89, fax: 93-487 32 27, <www.hcchotels.com>*. A mid-sized hotel in a handsome 1913 *modernista* townhouse on La Rambla de Catalunya. Rooms are standard and modern, renovated in 1997. Rooftop pool. Wheelchair access. 79 rooms.

San Medín € *Carrer de Gran de Gràcia 125, tel: 93-217 30 68, fax: 93-415 44 10, <www.sanmedin.com>*. There are few pensions in the Eixample, so this one just above the Diagonal in the Gràcia district is a discovery.

CIUTAT VELLA

Catalonia Albinoni €€€ *Portal de l'Àngel 17, tel: 93-318 41 41, fax: 93-301 26 31, <www.hoteles-catalonia.es>*. This charming hotel is housed in a stylish former palace on one of Barcelona's busiest pedestrian shopping streets, close to the Barri Gòtic, La Rambla and the Eixample. Rooms are large and well-furnished, and there's a very nice garden patio. It's a good choice if you want to be in the thick of things. Wheelchair access. 74 rooms.

Chic&basic €€ *Princesa 50, tel: 93-295 46 52, fax: 93-295 46 51, <www.chicandbasic.com>*. Latest on the scene, this stylish ultra-modern hotel is in a handsome 19th-century building, well located between the Ciutadella Park and the trendy Born area. Surprisingly good value. 39 rooms.

Colón €€€ *Avinguda de la Catedral 7, tel: 93-301 14 04, fax: 93-317 29 15, <www.hotelcolon.es>*. This is the closest you can get to the heart of the Barri Gòtic – right across the square from the cathedral. Sixth-floor rooms have large terraces; ask for one with a cathedral view if you make your reservation in time. Renovated in 1992, but the décor is already dated. The Colón has a comfortable, old-world feel to it and is one of the best-known hotels in the city. Wheelchair access. 147 rooms.

Cuatro Naciones €€ *La Rambla 40, tel: 93-317 36 24, fax: 93-302 69 85, <www.h4n.com>.* Long-established favourite on the lower half of La Rambla. This means nighttime noise, but being right in the heart of things. Bar/café. Parking. 34 rooms.

Hotel España €€–€€€ *Carrer de Sant Pau 11, tel: 93-318 17 58, fax: 93-317 11 34, <www.hotelespanya.com>.* Just off the lower part of La Rambla, the España may not be the place it once was, but it retains enough flavour of bygone days to recommend it. The beautiful public rooms were designed by *modernista* architect, Domènech i Montaner. Guest rooms are plain but clean and large. Wheelchair access. 85 rooms.

Gaudí €€€ *Carrer de Nou de la Rambla 12, tel: 93-317 90 32, fax: 93-412 26 36, <www.hotelgaudi.es>.* Opposite one of Gaudí's earliest works, the Palau Güell, and just off La Rambla. Clean, comfortable, simple rooms. Wheelchair access. 73 rooms.

Gran Hotel Barcino €€€ *Carrer de Jaume I 6, tel: 93-302 20 12, fax: 93-301 42 42, <www.hotelbarcino.com>.* Just off the Plaça de Sant Jaume, right in the heart of the Barri Gòtic, this modern hotel is chic and well designed. The large, airy lobby outclasses the rooms, though. Wheelchair access. 53 rooms.

Jardí €€ *Plaça Sant Josep Oriol 1, tel: 93-301 59 00, fax: 93-318 36 64, <www.hoteljardi-barcelona.com>.* Small hotel in the Barri Gòtic, overlooking two of the prettiest plazas in Barcelona. Jardí rooms are a bargain, although a plaza view costs a little more. Recently renovated and very popular so book well ahead. 42 rooms.

Neri €€€€ *Sant Sever, 5, tel: 93-304 06 55, fax: 93-304 03 37, <www.hotelneri.com>.* Elegant boutique hotel in a 17th-century palace looking over one of the Gothic quarter's most atmospheric squares near the cathedral. The roof terrace has views over medieval spires. Only 22 rooms.

Nouvel Hotel €€€ *Carrer de Santa Ana 18–20, tel: 93-301 82 74, fax: 93-301 83 70, <www.hotelnouvel.com>.* On a pedestrianised street between La Rambla and Portal d'Àngel, in an atmospheric area, this small hotel has a wonderful *modernista* lobby and dining room. Rooms are plain, but well equipped. Wheelchair access. 72 rooms.

Oriente €€€ *Rambla 45–47, tel: 93-302 25 58, fax: 93-412 38 19.* Nostalgic place and right on La Rambla. Built around a monastic complex, this was Barcelona's first official hotel. Ernest Hemingway and Hans Christian Anderson stayed here (but not together). Lots of character. Wheelchair access. 150 rooms.

Peninsular €€ *Carrer de Sant Pau 34, tel: 93-302 31 38, fax: 93-412 36 99.* In an old Augustian monastery, with rooms around an inner courtyard. Friendly, helpful staff and good value for money. 59 rooms.

Rembrandt € *Carrer de Portaferrisa 23, tel/fax: 93-318 10 11.* Clean and pleasant if somewhat basic, the family-run Rembrandt is on a pedestrianised street just off La Rambla. Accommodation is up several flights of stairs. Not all the rooms are en suite. 27 rooms.

Rialto €€€ *Carrer Ferrán 42, tel: 93-318 52 12, fax: 93-318 53 12, <www.gargallo-hotels.com>.* A small, modern and comfortable hotel located near Plaça Sant Jaume. Wheelchair access. 63 rooms.

Rivoli Rambla €€€€ *Rambla 128, tel: 93-481 76 76, fax: 93-317 50 53, <www.rivolihotels.com>.* Busy hotel right on La Rambla, close to the never-ending parade just beyond the front door. Smallish rooms. Fitness centre, jacuzzi, and solarium on the terrace. Frequent deals available. Wheelchair access. 90 rooms.

Roma Reial €–€€ *Plaça Reial 11, tel: 93-302 03 66, fax: 93-301 18 39.* The accommodation is basic but the situation, in this buzzing square, makes it a good, cheap option for those who like to be where the action is. 52 rooms.

San Agustí €€ *Plaça Sant Agustí 3, tel: 93-318 16 58, fax: 93-317 29 28.* A comfortable, traditional hotel in a pretty little square near the Rambla. Wheelchair access. 77 rooms.

Suizo €€€ *Plaça de l'Àngel 12, tel: 93-310 61 08, fax: 93-315 04 61, <www.gargallo-hotels.com>.* Close to the cathedral, and convenient for the Picasso Museum, this intimate, friendly hotel has a turn-of-the-20th-century air. Wheelchair access. 51 rooms.

Triunfo €€ *Passeig de Picasso 22, tel/fax: 93-315 08 60.* Basic but pleasant little *pension*, close to the lively nightlife of El Born, and overlooking Ciutadella Park. 15 rooms.

WATERFRONT (VILA OLÍMPICA)

Hotel Arts €€€€ *Passeig de la Marina 19–21, tel: 93-221 10 00, fax: 93-221 10 70, <www.ritzcarlton.com>.* The Hotel Arts is an high-tech, ultra-deluxe high-rise, situated right on the beach in Vila Olímpica. Extremely efficient, decorated with sophisticated, understated taste. Large rooms, huge bathrooms and amazing views of the Mediterranean and the city. Wheelchair access. 455 rooms.

DIAGONAL

Hotel Princess Sofía Intercontinental €€€€ *Plaça de Pius XII 4, tel: 93-508 10 00, fax: 93-508 10 01.* High-rise, luxury, four-star hotel in good location for business travellers, just off the Diagonal, near central business district. Less convenient for sightseers. Swimming pool. Wheelchair access. 505 rooms.

Hotel Rey Juan Carlos I €€€€ *Diagonal 661, tel: 93-364 40 40, fax: 93-364 42 64, <www.hrjuancarlos.com>.* A premier business choice, this huge five-star hotel at the west end of the Diagonal, offers every amenity a demanding guest could want. Several excellent restaurants, swimming pool and full health club. Wheelchair access. 505 rooms.

Recommended Restaurants

Dining out is a prime social activity in Barcelona. Catalan cooking is one of the finest regional cuisines in Spain, and there are many atmospheric restaurants that serve it in both hearty and haute versions. Barcelona's roster of Catalan and Spanish restaurants and tapas bars is now complemented by a wide selection of international and continental (and even fast food) restaurants. The best areas in which to eat are the Ciutat Vella, which includes the Barri Gòtic, El Raval and El Born, and the area around La Rambla; the Eixample district; and Barceloneta and the waterfront area near the Port Olímpic, which is where the most explosive recent growth has taken place.

Remember that local people eat lunch and dinner late *(see page 96)*. You can either join them in eating early-evening tapas, to stave off the hunger pangs, or go just after restaurants have opened, when foreign visitors are likely to be the only diners. (Many restaurants close between lunch and dinner. Those that do not are noted below.)

It's wise to make advance reservations, especially at the pricier establishments. The price guides below reflect the cost of an à la carte, three-course meal for one, with house wine.

€€€€	over 60 euros
€€€	30–60 euros
€€	20–30 euros
€	below 20 euros

CIUTAT VELLA

Agut €€ *Carrer Gignàs, 16, tel: 93-315 17 09.* Open daily for lunch and dinner (closed Mondays). This small, 75-year-old restaurant is hidden away on a small street in the Barri Gòtic. Relaxed and homely, it has plenty of Catalan flavour and lots of daily specials, which might include home-made cannelloni, fish or game. The excellent and huge rice dishes are meant to be shared.

Agut d'Avignon €€€–€€€€ *Carrer de la Trinitat, tel: 93-302 60 34.* Open daily for lunch and dinner (closed August). A 40-year-old, rustic restaurant in a small alley in the Barri Gòtic. The Catalan cooking is creative and hearty, the ambience informal, the prices high. Tremendous wine cellar.

Biocenter € *Carrer del Pintor Fortuny 25, tel: 93-301 45 83*. Open Mon–Sat for lunch, Wed–Sat for dinner. Vegetarian restaurant serving huge portions in a friendly atmosphere.

Cal Pep €€–€€€ *Plaça de les Olles 8, tel: 93-310 79 62*. Open Mon–Sat, lunch and dinner. A boisterous bar at the edge of La Ribera, near Santa María del Mar, this is the place for some of the best seafood in Barcelona – if you can get a seat. They don't take reservations, and there's just one row of chairs at the counter and a few tables in the back room. The counter is the place to be. The display of baby squid, octopus, fried fish, mussels and more is amazing.

Can Culleretes €–€€ *Carrer d'en Quintana 5, tel: 93-317 30 22*. Open Tues–Sat for lunch and dinner; Sun lunch only. Barcelona's oldest restaurant has served traditional Catalan food since 1786. It is cosy and informal, and serves classics like *espinacas à la catalana* (spinach with pine nuts and raisins) and *butifarra* (white sausage). Fixed-price menus available weekdays.

Los Caracoles €€–€€€ *Carrer d'Escudellers 14, tel: 93-302 31 85*. Open for lunch and dinner daily without interruption. 'The Snails' is famous for its chicken roasting on a spit outside, on one of the Old Quarter's busiest pedestrian streets. It has been around since 1835, and while it's touristy it is fun, and you can get a fine meal of fish, game, roasted chicken or lamb, in addition, of course, to snails.

Casa Leopoldo €€€ *Sant Rafael 24, tel: 93-441 30 14*. Open Tues–Sat for lunch and dinner; Sun lunch only. Just off the Rambla del Raval, this family-run restaurant serves excellent fish and is popular with those in the know.

La Casola € *Carrer de Sant Sever 3, tel: 93-318 15 80*. Open Mon–Wed for lunch only; Thurs–Fri lunch and dinner. Family-run establishment with good, simple home-cooked Catalan food.

La Cocotte Minute € *Passeig del Born 16, tel: 93-319 17 34.* Open Mon–Sat for lunch and dinner, Sun lunch only. Fifties decor and good, solid food at very reasonable prices in this youthful area.

Comme-Bio € *Via Laietana 28, tel: 93-319 89 68.* Open daily for lunch and dinner. Eat-all-you-want buffet as well as standard restaurant.

La Dolça Herminia €€ *Carrer de les Magdalenes 27, tel: 93-317 06 76.* Open daily for lunch and dinner. Close to Via Laietana, this smart but very reasonably priced establishment has an imaginative menu.

Egipte € *Rambla 79, tel: 93-317 95 45.* Open daily for lunch and dinner. Lively, good-value place on the main Rambla near La Boqueria market.

Restaurant España €–€€ *Carrer de Sant Pau 9, tel: 93-318 17 58.* Open for lunch and dinner daily. A good-value restaurant in the Hotel España, the dining room was decorated by *modernista* architect Domènech i Montaner, and the back room has murals by Ramón Casas, a contemporary of Picasso. There is a set-priced menu for both lunch and dinner that is good value, but it's almost worth going there for the associations and decor alone.

Freud B'Art €€€ *Baixada de Sant Miquel, 4, tel: 93-318 66 29.* Open Tues–Sat for dinner. Stylish decor with food to match in this restaurant/art gallery/cocktail bar.

El Gran Café €€–€€€ *Carrer d'Avinyó 9, tel: 93-318 79 86.* Open Mon–Sat for lunch and dinner. Looks like an English pub on the outside, but has a handsome *modernista* interior. The set menu is very good value, otherwise rather expensive.

Hofman €€€€ *Carrer de l'Argentería 74, tel: 93-319 58 89.* Open Mon–Fri for lunch and dinner. Seriously good food cooked by cordon bleu chefs in a cosy atmosphere. Booking essential. Expensive but worth it.

Juicy Jones € *Carrer del Cardenal Casañas 7, tel: 93-302 43 30*. Open daily. Just off the Rambla, serves good vegetarian/vegan dishes and fresh juices. A new branch just opened in Hospital.

Organic € *Junta de Commerç 11, tel: 93-301 09 02*. Open daily for lunch and dinner. Creative organic food in a large attractive space not far from La Rambla. They also have a popular take-away stall at the back of La Boqueria market for healthy fast food.

La Pizza Nostra € *Carrer Montcada, 29, tel: 93-319 90 58*. Open Tues–Sun for lunch and dinner. This small and friendly place just down the road from the Picasso Museum has a good selection of pizzas and pastas, some very creative.

Els Quatre Gats €€ *Carrer de Montsió 3, tel: 93-302 41 40*. Open Mon–Sat for lunch and dinner. 'The Four Cats', which was once the hangout of Picasso and friends, serves simple Catalan fare in fabulous *modernista* surroundings. It has a tapas menu and the *menú del día* is a good deal, but really the atmosphere's the thing.

Quo Vadis €€€€ *Carrer del Carme 7, tel: 93-302 40 72*. Open Mon–Sat for lunch and dinner. A long-time favourite of Barceloneses, especially opera-goers (the Liceu Opera House is only a couple of minutes away). With several small and elegant dining rooms, the feeling is intimate and relaxed, and the Spanish menu classy.

Senyor Parellada €€–€€€ *Carrer de l'Argentaría 37, tel: 93-310 50 94*. Open Mon–Sat lunch and dinner. An attractive, popular restaurant in La Ribera, close to the church of Santa Maria del Mar. Both the surroundings and the creative Catalan menu are sophisticated but unpretentious.

Taxidermista €€ *Plaça Reial 8, tel: 93-412 45 36*. The best choice in the plaza, this former taxidermist's premises has minimalist decor and imaginative food. The set lunch menu is particularly good value.

TAPAS BARS

Bar Pinotxo € *Mercat La Boqueria, La Rambla.* Open daily for breakfast and lunch. This tiny, plain-looking bar with a handful of stools is surrounded by La Boqueria's mesmerising produce. It's a terrific place to stop if you are shopping or sightseeing and your stomach's beginning to growl. The fish, as you would imagine, is incredibly fresh. Full lunch menu also available (recited orally, so it helps to know what some of the items are).

Euskal Etxea € *Placeta de Montcada 1–3, tel: 93-310 21 85.* Open Tues–Sat for lunch and dinner; Sun dinner only. A great Basque tapas bar with a huge choice that has quickly established itself as a firm local favourite.

Irati € *Carrer del Cardenal Casañas 17, tel: 93-200 69 53.* Open for lunch and dinner Tues–Sun. This immensely popular Basque tapas joint, just off La Rambla at the edge of the Barri Gòtic, is always packed. At lunchtime and in early evening, heaving trays of tapas (*pintxos* in Basque) are laid out on the bar. It's a bit like a party, except that you have to keep track of the number of tapas and the glasses of wine or beer you've had, and the cheerful attendants tally it all up before you leave.

El Xampanyet € *Carrer de Montcada 22, tel: 93-319 70 03.* Open daily 6.30–11.30pm. Situated near the Picasso Museum and El Born, this tiled bar specialises in cava (hence the name, which is Catalan for champagne) and some of the best tinned tapas in town, especially the anchovies.

WATERFRONT/PORT OLÍMPIC

Agua €€–€€€ *Passeig Marítim 30, tel: 93-225 12 72.* Open daily for lunch and dinner. Almost on the beach, with inside and outside tables, the modern and attractive Agua gets very busy, so booking is essential, especially if you want to sit on the terrace. Well-prepared fish, rice dishes such as risottos, and imaginative vegetarian dishes.

Can Ganassa €€ *Plaça de la Barceloneta 4, tel: 93-221 67 39.* Open Thur–Tues for lunch and dinner without interruption. A popular seafood restaurant on the main square in Barceloneta serving excellent fish dishes as well as a wide array of delicious tapas and sandwiches.

L'Elx al Moll €€–€€€ *Maremàgnum, Moll d'Espanya, local 9, tel: 93-225 81 17.* Open for lunch and dinner daily. A dependable seafood restaurant famed for its rice dishes from Valencia. Its terrace overlooking the fishing boats in the port is in one of the best positions you could wish for, almost like being at sea.

Lungomare Ristorante €–€€ *Carrer de la Marina 16–18, tel: 93-221 04 28.* Open Mon–Sat lunch and dinner; Sun lunch only (closed Sep). Overlooking the Olympic port, with views of yachts, this informal and unpretentious place has pizzas and pastas, as well as good, simple fish and meat dishes, and a handful of more exotic dishes.

Restaurante Set Portes €€€ *Passeig d'Isabel II 14, tel: 93-319 30 33.* Open daily for lunch and dinner without interruption. One of Barcelona's most venerable institutions, this has been a favourite for business meals and special occasions since 1836. Set Portes (meaning seven doors) is famous for its rice dishes; favourites include black rice with squid in its own ink and an assortment of paellas. Portions are very large, the dining rooms are elegant and the waiters are old-style attentive.

Talaia Mar €€€ *Carrer de la Marina 16, tel: 93-221 90 90.* Open daily for lunch and dinner. One of the best new examples of Barcelona's fascination with design, the Talaia Mar has a sweeping bay window overlooking the port. A creative Mediterranean and seafood menu, with a grilled fish of the day.

Xiringuíto Escribà €€€ *Avgda. Litoral Mar 42, Platja Bogatell, tel: 93-221 07 29.* Open Tues–Thur for lunch, Fri–Sun lunch and dinner; closed Mon. Lots of imaginative fish and rice dishes in this down-to-earth, family-run establishment, right by the beach.

And, yes, they are the same Escribà family that is renowned for their chocolates and pastries, so the puddings are guaranteed to be marvellous.

EIXAMPLE

La Bodeguita € *Rambla de Catalunya 100, tel: 93-215 48 94.* Open for lunch and dinner Tues–Sun. It's easy to pass by this simple *bodega* (next to Toni Miró's Groc fashion boutique) without even noticing it. Regulars pop in at any hour for *jamón serrano* (smoked ham) and a glass of Rioja. Good wine selection. No credit cards.

Casa Calvet €€€–€€€€ *Carrer de Casp 48, tel: 93-412 40 12.* Open Mon–Sat for lunch and dinner. Located on the ground floor of one of Antoni Gaudí's first apartment buildings, Casa Calvet exudes elegant *modernista* ambience. The service is extraordinary, and the tables are spaced well apart; some even occupy private booth areas. The Catalan menu is excellent and fairly priced.

Jaume de Provença €€€ *Carrer de Provença 88, tel: 93-430 00 29.* Open daily for lunch and dinner. This is reckoned to be among the best of the nouvelle cuisine restaurants in Barcelona and is correspondingly popular.

Madrid-Barcelona € *Carrer d'Aragó 282, tel: 93-215 70 26.* Open daily for lunch and dinner. Located just off Passeig de Gracia, this pleasantly old-fashioned place has a good selection of Catalan and regional Spanish dishes.

Mordisco € *Carrer del Rosselló 265, tel: 93-415 76 76.* Open daily for breakfast, lunch and dinner without interruption. Near the Eixample's major *modernista* sights and shopping, a convenient place for a fast lunch. Extensive list of sandwiches as well as more elaborate dishes. Friendly and efficient.

Taktika Berri €€–€€€ *Carrer de València 169, tel: 93-453 47 59.* Open for lunch and dinner daily without interruption. Basque cooking is the finest regional cuisine in Spain, and Basque restaurants are popping up everywhere. One of the best in Barcelona is this family-owned and operated tapas bar and restaurant in a converted textile workshop. The *pintxos* (tapas) are excellent, as are their creative entrées. Try the splendid desserts.

Tragaluz €€€ *Passatge de la Concepció 5, tel: 93-487 06 21.* Open daily for lunch and dinner. Barcelona's love affair with food comes to life in this trendy, colourful restaurant on a tiny passageway off Passeig de Gràcia. The main menu is creative, but there's also a selection of low-fat and veggie dishes, as well as a separate sushi restaurant downstairs.

ABOVE THE DIAGONAL

Bar Turó € *Tenor Viñas 1, Parc Turó, tel: 93-200 69 53.* Open daily for lunch and dinner, and all-day tapas. Tucked away in the upscale residential neighbourhood north of the Diagonal this joint is famed throughout the city. Good-value midday menu.

Botafumeiro €€€€ *Carrer Gran de Gràcia 81, tel: 93-218 42 30.* Open daily for lunch and dinner without interruption. This is Barcelona's top seafood restaurant and it is said to be the King of Spain's favourite. It's large and informal, with lots of action. Much of the fresh seafood is flown in daily from the owner's home territory, Galicia. You can get great shellfish and seafood *tapas* here (which keep costs down, if you're conscientious). To get a seat at the seafood bar, go at off-hours, earlier than local people would eat – noon–1pm for lunch, 7–8pm for dinner. Just north of the Diagonal, at the beginning of the Gràcia neighbourhood.

La Buena Tierra € *Carrer de l'Encarnació 56, tel: 93-219 82 13.* Open for lunch and dinner Mon–Sat. This vegetarian restaurant, located just north of the Travessera de Gracia, is quite handy if you've been to the Sagrada Família and are in need of instant sustenance. It's good for soups and mushroom-based dishes and it has a nice little garden (the restaurant's name means 'The Good Earth').

INDEX

Berlitz pocket guide

Barcelona

Twelfth Edition 2008

Written by Neil Schlecht
Updated by Judy Thomson
Edited by Pam Barrett
Series Editor: Tony Halliday

Printed in Singapore by Insight Print Services (Pte) Ltd, 38 Joo Koon Road, Singapore 628990. Tel: (65) 6865-1600. Fax: (65) 6861-6438

Berlitz Trademark Reg. U.S. Patent Office and other countries. Marca Registrada

Photography
AKG 15; Annabel Eston 11, 40, 79, 84; AP/empics 90; Mike Merchant 8, 41, 58, 69; Mark Read 6, 14, 17, 20, 24, 29, 30, 34, 39, 44, 47, 52, 53, 64, 66, 73, 76, 78, 92; Neil Schlecht 27, 45, 48, 50, 51, 83, 95; Bill Wassman 46, 65; Gregory Wrona 12, 18, 22, 25, 26, 28, 31, 32, 35, 37, 38, 49, 55, 57, 59, 60, 61, 62, 68, 70, 71, 72, 74, 77, 80, 86, 89, 93, 96, 98, 100.

Cover picture: Glen Allison/Alamy

Every effort has been made to provide accurate information in this publication, but changes are inevitable. The publisher cannot be responsible for any resulting loss, inconvenience or injury.

Contact us

At Berlitz we strive to keep our guides as accurate and up to date as possible, but if you find anything that has changed, or if you have any suggestions on ways to improve this guide, then we would be delighted to hear from you.

Berlitz Publishing, PO Box 7910, London SE1 1WE, England.
fax: (44) 20 7403 0290
email: berlitz@apaguide.co.uk
www.berlitzpublishing.com